LOVED TO LOVE
LOVING OTHERS AS JESUS HAS LOVED US

BY STEVE DEMME

Loved to Love

This book is dedicated to my ever
supportive, always faithful, loving wife
and my patient, forgiving, teachable
sons who learned along with me.

May it encourage all those families
whose hearts have been turned towards
God and towards each other.

May the Lord make you increase
and abound in love for one another and
for all" (1 Thessalonians 3:12)

LOVED TO LOVE

LOVING OTHERS AS JESUS HAS LOVED US

INTRODUCTION TO LOVED TO LOVE

This book is a part of a series of books on building a family of faith. My motivation in writing them is to pass on what I have learned in the past few years which has transformed my relationship with my heavenly Father and subsequently my wife and children. I began this journey by asking God to help me love Him with all my heart, soul, mind, and strength. In the book *Knowing God's Love* I share how God answered this prayer by first revealing His love for me.

One of the pivotal scriptures God quickened to my heart which spoke of His love was John 15:9. Jesus is speaking to His disciples, "As the Father has loved me, so have I loved you. Abide in my love." In meditating on this passage several truths have emerged. As much as the Father loved His Son, Jesus loves me the same way. Just writing those words continues to touch my heart.

I want to hold on to this truth, or as it says in the last four words of John 15:9 "Abide in my love." I began journalling to record the many and varied ways God was communicating to my heart so I would not forget what He had revealed. I also began studying scriptures reinforcing and expanding on God's love for each of His adopted children.

Then I noticed the key for maintaining this essential connection to the heart of God found in the next few verses. "If you keep my commandments, you will abide in my love, just as I have kept my Father's commandments and abide in His love. This is my commandment, that you love one another as I have loved you." (John 15:10, 12)

When I hear the words command or commandments my mind begins to think of things I have a duty to perform like tithing, sabbath keeping, Bible reading, etc. But I noticed the commandment Jesus is referring to is "to love one another as I have loved you." If I will love others, particularly my wife and children, as I have been loved, I will abide in the love of God. As a husband and father, my primary responsibilities are to love God, my wife, and my four sons. While many of the principles we will explore in this book are applicable to any believer, I am writing as a man and how God has led me to apply these principles to my family.

The fruit of loving others as we have been loved, will not only bless each of our homes, but our communities as well. In John 13, Jesus defines this approach as the "New Commandment" and as we practice and obey it, "all people" will know we are His disciples. "A new commandment I give to you, that you love one another: just as I have loved you, you also are to love one another. By this all people will know that you are my disciples, if you have love for one another." (John 13:34)

"May the Lord direct your hearts to the love of God and to the steadfastness of Christ." (2 Thessalonians 3:5)

Approach

Within the pages of this book we will be discussing the distinction between loving as we have been loved, and loving as we want to be loved. We will also talk about ways we can love our spouses and children as Jesus has loved us, which will provide insight into the new commandment. Beyond new insights into truth, I hope that we can simultaneously develop a new approach to being transformed by Jesus.

When I read a new book or receive new insights, my tendency is to seek ways to apply them. I begin with an upward vertical look at what God has revealed and then adopt a horizontal application to implement what I have been given. This may take the form of journalling or writing key insights on notecards and placing them in prominent locations like the refrigerator or as posting a sticky note on my computer.

The new command inspires a different technique and keeps my eyes up and focused on Jesus. This method leads to Christ being revealed in new ways as I fix my eyes on Him. "As I have loved you" continues to draw my attention to how I have been loved and am being loved by my savior. Transformation occurs by meditating on the person of Christ instead of the words of Christ.

I quickly acknowledge that I am unable to obey God, understand His love, or know how to apply truth without complete dependence on the Spirit. Just as Jesus was filled and empowered by the Spirit

to fulfill his mission on this earth, so must I be. The
flesh must die daily so that the Spirit can enable me
to "walk in love, as Christ loved us and gave Himself
up for us." (Ephesians 5:2)

Loving others as I have been loved must flow
from the heart. I can't fake sacrificial love. In order
to be obedient from the heart, I need to experience
ongoing transformation. As a father, I so wanted
to be able to teach my children to love God and His
word as He commands in Deuteronomy 6:7.

This concept was revealed in the order of
the verses in this significant portion of scripture
addressed to parents. Verse 7 commands me
to "teach them(His commands) diligently to your
children, and shall talk of them when you sit in your
house, and when you walk by the way, and when
you lie down, and when you rise." But this passage
follows the two previous commands for the teacher.
"You shall love the LORD your God with all your heart
and with all your soul and with all your might. And
these words that I command you today shall be on
your heart." (Deuteronomy 6:5-6) Before I can teach
my children I must first love God with all my heart,
and have His word on my heart.

Anyone who has taught knows the teacher
always benefits more than the students. This is part
of God's wise design He built into families. Even
though I have walked with God much longer than my
children, I am a disciple, a lifelong learner, who is
continually being changed into the image of Christ.
As I seek to disciple my family, I am being discipled.

For my message to be effective it must come from my heart and not from my head.

Loving God, and loving others as I have been loved, flows from understanding the good news of God's love expressed in the life and death of Jesus. The gospel is the power of God. "We love because He first loved us." (1 John 4:19) "God shows his love for us in that while we were still sinners, Christ died for us." (Romans 5:8) God has taken the initiative to love us. "God's love has been poured into our hearts through the Holy Spirit." (Romans 5:5)

As we keep our eyes looking to Jesus, our hearts open to the work of the Spirit, and comprehend with the saints "the love of Christ that surpasses knowledge," (Ephesians 3:19) we will be equipped to love as we have been loved, and be transformed in our extraordinary pilgrimage.

One of my favorite hymns is Turn Your Eyes Upon Jesus, by Helen Howarth Lemmel. The words from the chorus are a wonderful way to close this section, "Turn your eyes upon Jesus, look full in His wonderful face, and the things of earth will grow strangely dim, in the light of His glory and grace.

Since this book was first published, I have added a one hour talk on the same subject online. You may watch it here buildingfaithfamilies.org/lovedtolove/ Other material will continue to be added here in the future.

CHAPTER OVERVIEW

Chapter 1, Love Your Neighbor as Yourself, the Golden Rule, or the Royal Law, calls us to treat others as we desire to be treated. This concept, along with the Great Commandment, to love God with everything in us, is the basis and foundation for the law and the prophets.

The New Commandment is different. In this command, we are to love one another, **AS** Jesus has loved us. Instead of looking horizontally at others, we look up and seek to understand how God in Christ has loved us. This is the topic of **Chapter 2, The New Commandment**.

Chapter 3, AS, focuses on the key word in the New Commandment. This part of speech is a simile and used in comparisons. I first discovered this wonderful little word in John 15:9. "**AS** the Father has loved me, so have I loved you." Often I will substitute **AS** with **JUST AS** to make this comparison clearer.

Once we begin seeing this word and the concept of comparison in scripture, we begin to consider how Jesus has loved us. **Chapter 4, As the Father Has Loved Me, so Have I Loved You**, is full of wonderful passages which help us see how the Son of God has cared for us.

In **Chapter 5**, In this section, we zero in on how to "Love one another, as I have loved you." (John 15:12) This section is filled with practical ways God has helped me to apply this principle. Since all of the passages are from the four gospels this chapter is entitled The New Commandment in the

Gospels.

Love is an attitude as much as it is an act. Real love flows from within our hearts and not just what we do. As our hearts are changed, then our behavior will follow. Chapter 6, Transformed from Within, discusses this dynamic in more detail.

Chapter 7, The New Commandment in the Epistles, continues our search through the New Testament as we look for scriptures which apply this same command to love **AS** we have been loved.

We know we cannot hope to love from the heart without the help of the Spirit of God. Just as Jesus depended on the Spirit to help Him love us, so we too must rely on the Spirit to enable us to love the same way. **Chapter 8, Walk In the Spirit**, reveals the person and power of the Spirit to enable us to love as Jesus loved.

Chapter 9, Dying to Live, is written for husbands who are exhorted to love their wives, **AS** Christ loved the church. Jesus loved the church by laying His life down for her. As we men follow our Lord, we lose our life, and then find it. Life follows death, just as the resurrection followed the crucifixion.

Parents are the topic of the **Chapter 10, For Parents** We have addressed children, now we offer some tips for moms and dads, based on the relationship between Jesus and His Dad.

Chapter 11, The New Commandment and Me considers the good fruit which emerges as I adopt God's perspective on myself. This small chapter was hard to write. Most of us want to love God and others, but we often leave ourself out of the equation. But if God likes us, we ought to follow His lead and like ourself as well.

Chapter 12, Transformed in Love. This book is not a scriptural "How To" guide for Christians on how to act, but a new approach for discipleship. As we apply the new commandment and fix our attention on Jesus, our own visage will change as did the face of Moses when he was in the presence of God. Loving others as we have been loved, changes us.

Would you like to have the whole world know you are a disciple of Jesus the Christ? **Chapter 13, By This Shall All Men Know**, is all about two verses. "A new commandment I give to you, that you love one another: just as I have loved you, you also are to love one another. By this all people will know that you are my disciples, if you have love for one another." (John 13:34–35) Let's look to Jesus and change the world, beginning in our own family.

CHAPTER 1: LOVE YOUR NEIGHBOR AS YOURSELF

Several places in scripture, Jesus says "You shall love the Lord your God with all your heart and with all your soul and with all your mind." (Matthew 22:37) Then he says "And a second is like it: You shall love your neighbor as yourself." (Matthew 22:39)

This subsequent command to love others as ourself, or as we want to be loved, is referred to as the royal law, the golden rule, and is the fulfillment of the law and the prophets. Below are several of the scriptures speaking of this divine command.

"You shall not hate your brother in your heart, but you shall reason frankly with your neighbor, lest you incur sin because of him. You shall not take vengeance or bear a grudge against the sons of your own people, but you shall love your neighbor as yourself: I am the Lord." (Leviticus 19:17–18)

With God's help I have read the Bible through from Genesis to Revelation many times. I am always amazed when I discover hidden nuggets like Leviticus 19:17–18. I had assumed Jesus was the first one to teach us, "to love our neighbor as yourself," but here it is, in the middle of Leviticus.

"So whatever you wish that others would do to you, do also to them, for this is the Law and the Prophets." (Matthew 7:12)

"Owe no one anything, except to love each

other, for the one who loves another has fulfilled
the law. For the commandments, 'You shall not
commit adultery,' 'You shall not murder,' 'You
shall not steal,' 'You shall not covet,' and any other
commandment, are summed up in this word: 'You
shall love your neighbor as yourself.' Love does no
wrong to a neighbor; therefore love is the fulfilling
of the law." (Romans 13:8–10)

"If you really fulfill the royal law according to the
Scripture, 'You shall love your neighbor as yourself,'
you are doing well." (James 2:8)

"For the whole law is fulfilled in one word:
'You shall love your neighbor as yourself.'"
(Galatians 5:14)

"He said to him, 'You shall love the Lord your God
with all your heart and with all your soul and with all
your mind.' This is the great and first commandment.
And a second is like it: 'You shall love your neighbor
as yourself.' On these two commandments depend
all the Law and the Prophets." (Matthew 22:37–40)

This command to love others stimulates us to
think and reflect on how we desire to be loved. How
do we want to be treated? How do we want people
to speak to us? How do we like people to listen to us
when we are speaking? These are a few questions to
prompt our thinking. Personally I like to be treated
with respect. I like to be spoken to in an even tone
and not have people holler or use a loud voice when
addressing me. When I am speaking, I appreciate it
when my neighbor does not interrupt me but gives
me a chance to complete my thought.

Here a few more personal examples. One of my first jobs after high school, was working with a construction crew. The boss would give us instructions throughout the day, but without saying "please" and "thank you." The second in command was a bearded man who rode a motorcycle and wore a bandana. This rough looking guy would always add a respectful "please" when he asked us to do something, followed by an appreciative "thank you" when we completed the task. I have tried to follow his lead, regardless of the status of the people who work for me, because this is how I like to be treated.

As a student I always appreciated teachers who knew their subject well, were interesting, made the subject relevant, employed humor, and enjoyed what they were teaching. As a teacher, I try to teach as I liked being taught. Some call this edutainment, but to me this is simply applying the golden rule. I want my classes to be informative, fun, and applicable.

As a parishioner, I am edified by a preacher who sticks to the scriptures and is transparent about how the subject impacts him. When I teach/preach, I want the message to be thoroughly biblical as well as practical and real.

As a business man I appreciate it when customers pay their bills on time. When I owe money to vendors who provide a service to me, I endeavor to pay the invoice when it is presented and not wait the full thirty (30) days before sending a check. I understand this is not normal business practice, but if I am applying the golden rule, this is how I operate.

I take the passage literally, that the whole law and the prophets are built upon loving God and loving our neighbor as ourself. Since this is true, I have read through the ten commandments and selected the ones which seem to be pertaining to loving your neighbor. You shall not steal, bear false witness, murder, covet your neighbor's spouse or belongings, or commit adultery. There are many other commands flowing from this concept, like putting a railing around an open flat roof (Deuteronomy 22:8), or returning a wandering donkey or ox (Exodus 23:4).

Loving others this way encourages us to walk in our neighbors' shoes and see life from their perspective. We readily take care of ourselves, which is natural and human, but thinking of others takes some effort.

As a husband, I have observed how my wife and I are different. When I am sick, I just want to be left alone. I need rest, food, and a distraction in the form of good books or some good movies. I have discovered if I treat my wife as I desire to be treated, it does not work well.

For she does not like to be alone when she has an illness. Rather she needs to be comforted, play a game with me, have me rub her back, etc. In this case, I have to ask questions to discern how she would like me to serve her, and then put myself in her shoes.

Prayer

Father help us to love you with all our heart, soul, mind, and strength. And help us to love our neighbor well, by walking in their moccasins and putting their needs ahead of our own.

Note: In this revised edition, I have added questions to assist in processing the information in each chapter. Work through them for your own study, talk them out with your spouse, or study them in a small group setting, "for where two or three are gathered in my name, there am I among them." (Matthew 18:20) May God bless you on your journey to love others as you have been loved.

QUESTIONS FOR REFLECTION AND STUDY

1. Reflect on how you desire to be loved. Who has loved you well? How did they express their care for you? Be as specific as possible.
2. How do you like to be treated? Who treats you in this manner?
3. What behavior in your family, close friends, and even acquaintances and store clerks, makes you feel valued and loved?
4. Next ask yourself, do I act and talk this way to others? Write down a few ways you would like to change in this area.
5. What scripture caught your attention as you read this chapter? Why?

CHAPTER 2:
THE NEW COMMANDMENT

In 2012, a wonderful passage in John 15:9 was illuminated to my heart. Jesus says, "as the Father has loved me, so have I loved you." As much as His Dad loves Him, He loves me the same way. This one verse, more than any other, made me know God not only loves me, He likes me. In another book *Knowing God's Love*, I wrote extensively about how our Dad has adopted us and made us His children.

As I meditated on this scripture, I noticed a new commandment that follows this wonderful revelation. It is found in verse 12 of the same chapter. "This is my commandment, that you love one another as I have loved you." (John 15:12) This commandment was first mentioned and named in John 13:34: "A new commandment I give to you, that you love one another: just as I have loved you, you also are to love one another."

The Golden Rule instructs us to love our neighbor as we want to be loved. The New Commandment directs us to love others as we have been loved. This is a significant distinction and one which I did not readily comprehend before.

To apply the new commandment, I don't think about myself or how I want to be loved, instead I think of Jesus and how He has loved and always loves me. Then I love others the same way. As followers of Jesus, we are to love others as we have been loved, not as we want to be loved.

To summarize John 15, verses 9 and 12; As the

Father has loved Jesus, so has Jesus loved us. As Jesus has loved us, we are to love each other. As I meditated on this wonderful "New" commandment I sought to know more of how Jesus has loved us. I began to document all the ways my Savior loves me. Appendix A is my attempt to collate many of these passages. My heart was filled with gratitude as I pondered all the different ways I have been, and am being, loved by Jesus. He not only died for me, He prays for me, serves me, heals me, and provides for me. As I take into account the ways I have been loved, then I am in a better position to love my wife and children the same way.

"A new commandment I give to you, that you love one another: just as I have loved you, you also are to love one another." (John 13:34)

The Upward Look

The primary difference between the commandment to love my neighbor as myself, and the new commandment, is where I am looking. In loving my neighbor as myself, I consider how I want to be loved or how my neighbor wants to be loved. I am focusing on myself and my neighbor.

With the new commandment, I am focused on Jesus. All my attention is fixed on Christ. The best part of studying the life and person of Jesus, and learning how He has loved and is loving us, is knowing Him more. Moses said, "Show me now your ways that I may know you." (Exodus 33:13) As I learn more about His ways, I am learning more about Him.

His character and personality are being revealed to me in new and deeper ways.

Transformation

Before I delve into how Jesus has loved us, there is another significant fruit I want to mention. As we fix our attention on Jesus, we are not only learning more about Him, we are becoming more like Him. The best illustration I know of, which describes the benefits of this upward looking approach is found in a short story published by Nathaniel Hawthorne in 1850, called "The Great Stone Face." I cannot do justice to the story in just one paragraph, so I urge you to read it for yourself in the Appendix.

The story is about a boy who grows up next to the mountains, where there is an image of a wise, noble face, easily observed in the unique rock formation on the face of a mountain. The prophecy declared that one day a man would be born within sight of this rock formation who would grow up to be a noble man himself. Not only would he be a great and wise man, but he would have the same visage as the man on the mountain face. I hate to spoil the story, but the boy devoted himself to staring at the stone face and meditating on the wonderful character of this coming hero. After a lifetime of gazing at the mountain and thinking about what kind of sterling character that man would be, the boy became the man and fulfilled the prophecy. He not only looked like the stone face; he had the corresponding character. Please read this wonderful piece of literature by Nathaniel Hawthorne to receive the full impact.

I believe Scripture corroborates this concept of focusing our attention on who we want to be instead of how we want to act. We become what we love. "Like grapes in the wilderness, I found Israel. Like the first fruit on the fig tree in its first season, I saw your fathers. But they came to Baal-peor and consecrated themselves to the thing of shame, and became detestable like the thing they loved." (Hosea 9:10) The Israelites were changed into the image of the detestable thing they loved. We become what we set our affections on.

This principle can be discouraging or put the fear of God into us, but it can also give us hope, for the more we fix our gaze on Jesus, the more like Him we shall become. We will be transformed into His likeness. "We all, with unveiled face, beholding the glory of the Lord, are being transformed into the same image from one degree of glory to another. For this comes from the Lord who is the Spirit." (2 Corinthians 3:18)

The background for Paul's illustration in 2 Corinthians 3 comes from Moses meeting God in the wilderness. After they left Egypt, Moses spent considerable time on the mountain in the presence of God. When he descended to the camp of the Israelites, it was necessary for him to cover his face with a veil because his face shone. "Whenever Moses went in before the Lord to speak with him, he would remove the veil, until he came out. And

when he came out and told the people of Israel
what he was commanded, the people of Israel would
see the face of Moses, that the skin of Moses' face
was shining. And Moses would put the veil over
his face again, until he went in to speak with him."
(Exodus 34:34-35) When Moses was in the presence
of God he was transformed. God is light, and this
light was reflected on the face of Moses.

There will come a day when we shall see
Jesus face to face. The results will be beyond our
imagination. "Beloved, we are God's children now,
and what we will be has not yet appeared; but we
know that when he appears we shall be like him,
because we shall see him as he is." (1 John 3:2)

The Glory of God

The most effective way to become more like
Jesus is to spend time in His presence, reading His
word, communing with Him, and meditating on His
character. Instead of seeking the character qualities
of Jesus, let us seek Jesus Himself. "God, who
said, 'Let light shine out of darkness,' has shone
in our hearts to give the light of the knowledge
of the glory of God in the face of Jesus Christ."
(2 Corinthians 4:6)

Just as the boy sitting on his front porch would
think about the Great Stone Face, some mornings I
meditate on the Godly character qualities which are
present in Jesus, the incarnate Son of God. For God's
Son is the word, made flesh. He is the living example
of love, the embodiment of the fruits of the Spirit,

and the eternal wisdom that comes from above. As I consider the different facets of the character of Jesus, I am increasing my knowledge of His nature and being transformed in the process. This upward look is what differentiates the new commandment from the second commandment.

Daily Devotions

Since 1976 I have made a habit of reading scripture daily, compassing the Bible from Genesis to Revelation once each year. I find my heart is softened as I am exposed to the inspired passages. Anointed words of life are true heart food. My faith has also been increased for "faith comes from hearing, and hearing through the word of Christ." (Romans 10:17). After reading the word, I set aside time to pray, beginning with my family I also pray for others. In 2012, I began creating topical Bible studies to help transform my thinking.

After several years and many studies (over 100), the Good Spirit whispered the words to my hear. "spirit and truth." That phrase comes from the conversation between Jesus and the Samaritan woman at the well.

"The hour is coming, and is now here, when the true worshipers will worship the Father in spirit and truth, for the Father is seeking such people to worship him. God is spirit, and those who worship him must worship in spirit and truth." (John 4:23–34)

He affirmed my knowledge of truth, but gently made me know I needed to develop "the spirit" or my relational connection with God. I began to take regular thirty minute walks around my neighborhood. I find when I am sitting in my comfy chair, I am prone to drowsiness and distraction. When I walk I am able to focus my attention on communing with God alone. My heart and spirit are encouraged in this precious time with the living God.

I like the word communing for sometimes I talk, other times I listen. God faithfully meets me as I seek Him. Reading scripture increases my knowledge "about" God, communing daily is increasing my knowledge "of" God, or as Peter exhorts, "grow in the grace and knowledge of our Lord and Savior Jesus Christ." (2 Peter 3:18)

While attending seminary I had the opportunity to rent a room in the home of Elisabeth Elliot. By interacting with her on a daily basis, eating meals, doing chores, attending church together, I got to know her as a person, and not a famous speaker and author. Now, when I read her books or listen to a recorded talk, I receive so much more from what she says because I recognize her voice and know her heart.

The God in the Bible is my Dad. He is alive. I enjoy spending time learning about Him in the past, and I am so grateful for opportunities to experience His presence in the present. My reading of the written word is enhanced by knowing the living word.

If you have been reading my monthly newsletters or heard me speak in the past, you know I have struggled to "wait on God" for I had difficulty believing His grace and how much He truly cared for me. It is only in the past few years I have become convinced that God not only loves me, but likes me. I think if He had whispered "spirit and truth" five years ago I would not have known how to respond.

Believing God is beaming when I draw near to Him makes it so much easier to approach Him. I know He genuinely enjoys my company. He is my Dad. He knows me intimately and still affectionately desires hanging out with me. I know this from the source of truth, the holy scripture, which says "God is for me" (Psalm 56:9) and Jesus said, "As the Father has loved me, so have I loved you." (John 15:9)

David certainly had a wonderful connection with the Almighty. "Oh, taste and see that the Lord is good! Blessed is the man who takes refuge in him!" (Psalms 34:8) His inspired words encourage me to move beyond seeing God from afar, but getting close while tasting His goodness.

Seeking God

In the fall of 2018, I was having my morning "walk with God." Normally, I begin by confessing sins while remembering God's promise of forgiveness, "If we confess our sins, He is faithful and just to forgive us our sins and to cleanse us from all unrighteousness." (1 John 1:9)

Then I generally recite a scripture about God's nearness to help me believe that God is findable, "Come close to God and He will come close to you." (James 4:8 NLT)

I especially like the passage that encompasses both of these thoughts. God cleanses from sin and makes me near through the blood of Jesus: "In Christ Jesus you who once were far off have been brought near by the blood of Christ." (Ephesians 2:13)

Come into His Presence

On this particular fall morning, the Spirit of God led me to approach God in a new way through several phrases which are found in Psalm 100. The first was, "Come into His presence with singing!" So, I began to sing (silently) as I walked on the sidewalk. I sang all four verses of "Rejoice the Lord is King." This was exhilarating. I felt like I was already joining the angels as I began with worship instead of humble confession and working my way into God's presence. My spirit was already encouraged.

Enter into His Gates with Thanksgiving

The next phrase which was quickened to me was "Enter His gates with thanksgiving". Then I began to give thanks. I had to work at this a little, for it was a departure from my normal routine of confession, cleansing, seeking, etc. However, once I got with the new program it was a wonderful time. I spent several minutes giving thanks, and the more I exercised my thank muscles, the more things I thought of for which to be thankful.

At first, I was thankful for the sunshine, my family, and practical items. Then I began to be thankful for who God is, and what He has done for me. I thanked Him for loving and liking me, for cleansing me from sin, for clothing me in the righteousness of Jesus. Once I developed some momentum, my perspective on the day had already changed. I felt rich!

Bless His Name

The third portion of the Psalm that was illuminated that morning was, "Bless His Name." I took this to mean I was to praise God for who He is. I had begun by coming into His presence God with singing, then by entering His gates with thanksgiving, and now I had the opportunity and privilege to give Him honor and bless Him for His character and nature.

My experience was similar to what happened when I gave thanks. As I pondered and thought about the nature of God, my heart and mind reveled in what I knew about Him, and the thoughts turned from a trickle into a stream.

God is Love.

"We have come to know and to believe the love that God has for us.
God is love, and whoever abides in love abides in God, and God abides in him."
(1 John 4:16)

God is Light.

"God is light, and in him is no darkness at all."
(1 John 1:5)

God is Good.

"Taste and see that the LORD is good! Blessed
is the man who takes refuge in him!"
(Psalms 34:8)

God is Near.

"He is actually not far from each one of us, for
'In him we live and move and have our being.'"
(Acts 17:27–28)

Since those first few days applying these
principles, when I thought of many characteristics
of God, now I try to focus on one aspect of God's
nature and chew on it for several minutes.

Give Me Ears to Hear

After I have progressed through this edifying
sequence, I then ask God to give me ears to
hear what His Spirit is saying to me. He faithfully
communicates with me and leads me in different
directions. Some days I pray for others. Other days
I continue to ruminate on the character of God. The
one constant is that I sense I am in God's presence
and that we are communing.

One afternoon I was walking on the home stretch
and could see our house in the distance. With a
hymn playing in my mind, along with a thankful
heart, I began to think about the words of Jesus in
Matthew 11:28–29. "Jesus said, 'Come to me, all of
you who are weary and carry heavy burdens, and I
will give you rest. Take my yoke upon you. Let me
teach you, because I am humble and gentle at heart,
and you will find rest for your souls.'"

I had a deep desire to be "humble and gentle at heart" so my grandchildren would find rest and safety when they were with me. Three of my grandchildren are foster boys and have experienced much trauma. I so wanted them to be at peace. This is such lovely fruit, that flows from focusing and meditating on Jesus.

In hindsight, I see that when God taught me about the "new commandment", my attention was directed to Jesus. When He subsequently led me to seek Him according to the order found in Psalm 100, my attention was again pointed to Jesus. I have learned so much about Jesus not just by reading a passage about Him, or by rattling off names for Him, (Good Shepherd, Light of the World, etc.) but by taking time to contemplate and give my full attention for several minutes to thinking about Him.

I am engaged on this quest to see God for who He truly is, and not who I thought He was, or how I mistakenly perceived Him. I recognize that my understanding of God has been shaped by knowledge received from my parents, my pastor, books I have read, and sermons I have heard. Truth is transforming my mind and heart. Coupled with the systematic exposure to sacred Scriptures, I am also tasting, seeing, and experiencing the presence of the Living God during the rhythm of my morning walks.

The more time I spend with God, the more I love Him. The more I love Him, the greater my desire to know Him. St. Augustine expresses this so eloquently when he writes, "To fall in love with

God is the greatest romance; to seek Him the greatest adventure; to find Him, the greatest human achievement."

Ordering Your Way Rightly

After practicing this new discipline, I sensed the Spirit saying, "orders his way rightly." When I returned home, I looked up this phrase. "The one who offers thanksgiving as his sacrifice glorifies me; to one who orders his way rightly I will show the salvation of God!" (Psalms 50:23) This was a confirmation to me, of the value and effectiveness of seeking God this way.

If this approach for coming into His presence as found in Psalm 100 resonates with your heart, check back to our website for more information at BuildingFaithFamilies.org or listen to podcasts 209–216 at the same location.

Prayer

We echo the request of the Greeks at the feast who asked Philip, "Sir, we would see Jesus." (John 12:20-21) Give us "the Spirit of wisdom and of revelation in the knowledge of Him." (Ephesians 1:17) Amen.

QUESTIONS FOR REFLECTION AND STUDY

1. Jesus declares in John 15:9, As the Father has loved me, so have I loved you. What are some ways Jesus demonstrated his love towards people he met on earth? How has He demonstrated his love to you? List as many examples as you can think of.

2. Jesus says just a few verses later in John 15:12, This is my commandment, that you love one another as I have loved you. He's passing on the baton to us! What is the difference between the second commandment (discussed in chapter 1) and this new commandment?

3. If you have time, read Nathaniel Hawthorne's story, "The Great Stone Face," in the Appendix. Think about Hosea 9:10 and 2 Corinthians 3:18, as you do. Is it true that people become like the person or thing they love and admire?

4. Which character qualities of Jesus are your favorite? Why?

5. Read Psalm 100. Do you see the character qualities of God sandwiched in between the three steps of singing, giving thanks, and blessing His name? (Hint: They are verses 3 and 5.)

6. What is the greatest human achievement, according to St. Augustine?

CHAPTER 3:
"AS"

When I think of the new command, I think of one word–"as". AS is a simile, which is an expression of comparison. When I think of a simile, I think of two words or phrases which are similar. A simile is similar.

When using a figure of speech for comparison, two key words are employed, "as" and "like." Of the two, "as" is the word which makes the comparison more explicit, while "like" is more general. I sometimes add a few words "just as" and "kinda like" to differentiate As and Like.

Jesus taught using similes on several occasions.

"Behold, I am sending you out AS sheep in the midst of wolves, so be wise AS serpents and innocent AS doves." (Matthew 10:16)

"For JUST AS Jonah was three days and three nights in the belly of the great fish, so will the Son of Man be three days and three nights in the heart of the earth. (Matthew 12:40)

"Be merciful, even AS your Father is merciful." (Luke 6:36)

"AS Moses lifted up the serpent in the wilderness, so must the Son of Man be lifted up." (John 3:14)

The Apostle Paul used this figure of speech while writing to the churches.

"Be imitators of me, AS I am of Christ." (1 Corinthians 11:1)

"To the Jews I became AS a Jew, in order to win Jews. To those under the law I became AS one under the law (though not being myself under the law) that I might win those under the law." (1 Corinthians 9:20)

"Do not rebuke an older man but encourage him AS you would a father, younger men AS brothers, older women AS mothers, younger women AS sisters, in all purity." (1 Timothy 5:1-2)

The simile is very effective in making comparisons in the gospels and the letters to the churches. When it is used in John 13 and 15, it lifts our attention heavenward and causes us to consider how we have been loved perfectly and eternally by God.

The new commandment is vertical in nature, while the second commandment is horizontal. In seeking to obey the second command we think how we would like to be loved and then do the same for others. We look into our own heart and then consider others, which is helpful, but we don't look to God. The new commandment directs our attention upward to Jesus and we ponder how He loved us.

AS is the pivotal word in John 13:34, 15:9, and 15:12. In John 15:9, "AS the Father has loved me, so have I loved you." In John 13:34 and again in John 15:12, Jesus says that we are to love one another AS we have been loved by Him. Here is the first part of John 15:9 with the memory aid; "(Just) AS the Father has loved me, so have I loved you."

The new commandment places our focus on how the Father loved Jesus and how Jesus loved us as the model for how we are to love one another. Let me give you an illustration of how this has changed my thinking and subsequently my behavior.

Husbands

I know there is a movement in some circles, to counteract the inroads of radical feminism in the church by emphasizing men being masculine. Verses like Ephesians 5:22, "Wives, submit to your own husbands, as to the Lord." are frequently quoted. When I heard this scripture exposited I concluded it was my responsibility as a husband to ensure my wife was submissive. Because of my understanding of the new commandment I no longer hold this view. Before you throw the book down, give me a chance to explain please.

Ephesians 5:25, "Husbands, love your wives, **AS** Christ loved the church and gave himself up for her," is the primary passage most men will quote when they are asked to choose one scripture which articulates their responsibility in marriage. In reading these inspired words, I see the new commandment principle in Paul's words "love your wives, **AS** Christ loved the church." "Love one another, **AS** I have loved you." The language is remarkably similar. I am to love my wife, **AS** Jesus loves me or **AS** He loved the church.

Submission

With my newly acquired insight into the new commandment, I rethought the verses on submission and asked myself, "How did Jesus love me?" There is a big difference between having Jesus as my Savior and Jesus as my Lord. As a disciple, believer, and follower of Jesus I have asked Him to be my Savior and Lord. How did I arrive at the place where I wanted Jesus to have the last say in my life? What compelled me to submit to Christ? Did He make me submit to Him? I know He could have, but He didn't. Instead He chose to humble Himself, lay His life down for me, pray for me, and wash my feet. In the process He won my heart and I found I wanted to submit to Him. He didn't forcibly impose His will or use His authority to rule over me, rather He used His power and position to serve me and build me up. And if I am to love my wife **AS** Jesus loved me, how can I emulate this same strategy of Christ towards Sandi?

I now am convinced it is not my responsibility to use my position and authority to ensure my wife submits, my calling is to love her, **AS** Christ loved me. He laid His life down for me. He took the initiative and loved me while I was a messy sinner. Seeing scripture through the lens of loving others **AS** I have been loved, has been incredibly enlightening. I don't wait for my wife to become submissive before I like her, nor do I only love my children when they are honoring and respectful. I love them regardless of whether they are compliant or lovable, because this is my calling. I will share more insights on the new command in marriage later in the book.

As I pondered the passage for wives to submit, I realized this verse is directed to her not me, "Wives,

..." My responsibility is to love **AS** I have been loved. Whether she chooses to submit or not, is up to her. How she responds to scripture is not my department nor my responsibility.

AS the Father has sent me

I was sharing some of these insights from John 15 with a friend who is a devoted Christian. She was bemoaning her unmarried state, wondering why she didn't have a husband and children. She questioned why she worked so hard for so little money (at a Christian School), and was having a splendid pity party. While attending a worship service, she joined in singing a hymn with the phrase, "**AS** the Father has sent me, so send I you" taken from John 20:21, and her sadness lifted. She recognized she was doing what Jesus had done in laying His life down for others. Her sadness was replaced with joy and renewed courage, for she was following the steps her master had trod.

Jesus is Patient

I have a son with Downs Syndrome who lives with us. He has a sweet spirit, and moves more slowly than I do. This afternoon we were taking down the Christmas lights together and he needed a warmer coat and some gloves. This would have taken me two minutes, but it took him about ten, or so it seemed. At first, I thought about all the times he has patiently waited for me, which brought a measure of peace. Then I thought about Jesus who was patient and kind. Instead of overcoming my impatience by thinking horizontally, I was helped to see Jesus and be patient, for Jesus is patient. I am starting to grasp the new command and how it applies to life with those I love.

When I am reading scripture I continue to find the word "as" appearing throughout the New Testament. To summarize, here are several passages which incorporate the spirit of the new command. I took the liberty of capitalizing the word **AS**.

"Therefore welcome one another **AS** Christ has welcomed you, for the glory of God." (Romans 15:7)

"Be kind to one another, tenderhearted, forgiving one another, **AS** God in Christ forgave you." (Ephesians 4:32)

"Forgiving each other; **AS** the Lord has forgiven you, so you also must forgive." (Colossians 3:13)

"Be imitators of God, as beloved children. And walk in love, **AS** Christ loved us and gave himself up for us, a fragrant offering and sacrifice to God." (Ephesians 5:1-2)

These scriptures have the specific word **AS** in them which makes them easy to find. They also directly relate to some act of Christ. We are to welcome each other because Christ Jesus welcomed us. We are to be kind, forgiving, and tenderhearted for this is how we each were treated. We are exhorted to walk in love as Jesus loved us and gave Himself for us.

Here are the referenced verses.

"A new commandment I give to you, that you love one another: just **AS** I have loved you." (John 13:34)

"**AS** the Father has loved me, so have I loved you. Abide in my love." (John 15:9)

"This is my commandment, that you love one another **AS** I have loved you." (John 15:12)

"Jesus said to them again, 'Peace be with you. **AS** the Father has sent me, even so I am sending you.'" (John 20:21)

Prayer

"Since we are surrounded by so great a cloud of witnesses, let us also lay aside every weight, and sin which clings so closely, and let us run with endurance the race that is set before us, looking to Jesus, the founder and perfecter of our faith," (Hebrews 12:1–2)

QUESTIONS FOR REFLECTION AND STUDY

1. In your own words write out the difference between "as" and "like" which is mentioned at the beginning of this chapter.

2. The second commandment and the new commandment: one is vertical and one is horizontal. Which is which? Write it out in a way that establishes it clearly in your mind.

3. Steve was applying this principle to the husband-wife relationship. If you are a husband, think about what God says to you (Ephesians 5:25). If you are a wife, think about what God says to you (Ephesians 5:22). Describe how your heart attitude and your behavior reflects the concept of "loving **AS** Christ loved the church" or "submitting **AS** to the Lord."

4. Describe how Jesus lovingly compels us to submit to Him.

5. Steve lists a few of the verses in the New Testament with **AS** which directly relate to an act of Christ and call us to emulate His behavior. Use these, and add to them if you can. Make a list and/or do a study of ways that the church is called to act toward others(beginning with our spouse and children) **AS** Jesus acted toward us.

CHAPTER 4:
AS THE FATHER
HAS LOVED ME

Since 2012 I have thought often of John 15:9, "As the Father has loved me, so have I loved you. Abide in my love." I have wondered about the relationship between the Father and the Son, and how the Father loved the Son. As I searched the scriptures, I discovered over one hundred verses in the Gospel of John where Jesus speaks of His Father. These passages reveal a glimpse into their relationship. Here is a short excerpt of how the Father loved the Son.

At His baptism Jesus was verbally affirmed by His Dad.

"When Jesus was baptized, immediately he went up from the water, and behold, the heavens were opened to him, and he saw the Spirit of God descending like a dove and coming to rest on him; and behold, a voice from heaven said, 'This is my beloved Son, with whom I am well pleased.'" (Matthew 3:16–17)

The Father encouraged His Son in the presence of His disciples.

"Behold, a bright cloud overshadowed them, and a voice from the cloud said, 'This is my beloved Son, with whom I am well pleased; listen to him.'" (Matthew 17:5)

He aways hears His Son's prayers.

Jesus was at the tomb of Lazarus. "So they took away the stone. And Jesus lifted up his eyes and said, "Father, I thank you that you have heard me. I knew that you always hear me." (John 11:41–42)

The Father taught the Son.

"Jesus said to them, 'When you have lifted up the Son of Man, then you will know that I am he, and that I do nothing on my own authority, but speak just as the Father taught me.'" (John 8:28)

It is a worthwhile exercise to meditate on and contemplate on how the Father loved the son for two reasons. One, this is a perfect model for any father/son relationship. If you want to know what the ideal Dad looks like, look at the Father in heaven. If you want to know the perfect son, consider Jesus. The way they interacted is precious and unparalleled. The Father comes to His Son's baptism, a big event with lots of folks around, and says, "This is my boy. He is a great son and I am totally pleased with him." Later, on the mountain, he says similar words and then tells the disciples to "listen to him." You could go right down the list of scriptures and apply them to your parenting. They have mutual admiration and respect for each other. They work together, listen to each other, trust each other, and are in absolute unity. It is the perfect picture of what a family should look like.

The second reason is that in the same manner that Jesus was loved, He loves us, which is the purpose of this book. "As the Father has loved me, so have I loved you." (John 15:9)

So Have I Loved You.

Jesus loves us, just as He was loved by His Dad. He learned what love was from His Heavenly Father and now showers us with the same perfect affection and care. One afternoon I was thinking of how God loves me. A river of thoughts poured through my heart and mind. I reflected on Jesus becoming human, providing healing, and hearing my prayers. I pictured Him kneeling and humbly washing the disciple's feet. I thought of how He forgave my sins even at the expense of dying for them, and He now sits at the right hand of the Father praying for me.

As soon as I could put pen to paper I sought to record all the thoughts which flowed through my consciousness. Then I sought accompanying scriptures and during the course of my Bible reading over the next few years, I continued to add to my list. I regularly read these passages which increase my knowledge of the love of God as well as inspiring worship and gratitude.

The rest of this chapter is made up of a few of the scriptures I consider exclusively within the realm of Jesus focusing on the many ways He loves us. My list is by no means exhaustive, and half the fun was assembling it in the first place. I hope you will study them, and be inspired to make your own lists. I am happy to prime the pump and inspire more study of the scripture. There is nothing better than mining the depths of scripture for oneself. I remember and retain so much more when I do my own digging. Here are a few to get you started, the rest are in Appendix A.

He was pierced, crushed, and wounded for us.
"He was pierced for our transgressions; he was crushed for our iniquities; with his wounds we are healed." (Isaiah 53:5)

He is with us always.
"I am with you always, even unto the end of the world." (Matthew 28:20)

He takes away our sin.
"Behold, the Lamb of God, who takes away the sin of the world." (John 1:29)

He sends the Spirit to be with us forever.
"I will ask the Father, and he will give you another Helper, to be with you forever." (John 14:16)

He lives in us.
"I have been crucified with Christ. It is no longer I who live, but Christ who lives in me." (Galatians 2:20)

He grants us the gift of eternal life.
"The wages of sin is death, but the free gift of God is eternal life in Christ Jesus our Lord." (Romans 6:23)

He delivers us from condemnation.
"There is therefore now no condemnation for those who are in Christ Jesus." (Romans 8:1)

He never changes.
"Jesus Christ is the same yesterday and today and forever." (Hebrews 13:8)

He brings us to God.
"Christ also suffered once for sins, the righteous for the unrighteous, that he might bring us to God, being put to death in the flesh but made alive in the spirit." (1 Peter 3:18)

Prayer

Dear God, help us to "Walk in love, as Christ loved us and gave himself up for us, a fragrant offering and sacrifice to God." (Ephesians 5:2)

QUESTIONS FOR REFLECTION AND STUDY

1. How did the Father encourage and affirm His Son?
2. What are the 2 reasons to meditate on how the Father loved the Son.
3. How can this be a model for your relationship with your parents / children?
4. How can studying how the Father loved Jesus help us to love others?
5. Consider the list of ways Jesus shows his love for us (some in the chapter and the rest in Appendix A). Brainstorm several ways you could meditate on these truths and the supporting verses. Perhaps once a day, at the beginning of a meal? As you get in your car to drive to work? As you climb into bed at night?

CHAPTER 5:
THE NEW COMMANDMENT IN THE GOSPELS

The highest purpose and ultimate goal for each of God's children is to love God, know God, and be transformed into His image. I fervently hope these passages and my comments will not be treated as a self-help guide for "How To Love Others" or "How to Apply the New Commandment." It is my hope God will answer the prayer of Paul, "that the God of our Lord Jesus Christ, the Father of glory, may give you the Spirit of wisdom and of revelation in the knowledge of Him." (Ephesians 1:17)

My comments center around how God has led me to understand and apply these scriptures. Only the word of God is inspired and I trust each reader will ask God to write these sacred words on their heart and lead them to an understanding of how to put them into practice. As my primary responsibility is to my wife and children, much of what I write is in the context of my family.

In his pastoral letter to Timothy, Paul teaches, under the direction of the Spirit, how the pastor is to relate to the members of his flock. "Do not rebuke an older man but encourage him as you would a father, younger men as brothers, older women as mothers, younger women as sisters, in all purity." (1 Timothy 5:1-2) Notice each of these church relationships is tied to a family relationship. We learn how to relate to older men, by how we treat our dad.

Younger men are to be thought of as siblings. So too with the women in the body of Christ. We are instructed how to relate to the larger body of Christ, by how we relate to our parents and siblings. A heathy church is the result of each of the members first living out the new commandment within their own home.

The following passages are key scriptural concepts I am earnestly seeking to apply in my home. I pray this book will be practical. Each of these verses were chosen as concrete examples of how to love others as we have been loved.

He is always approachable.

"Come to me, all who labor and are heavy laden, and I will give you rest." (Matthew 11:28)

I want to be in a good place of resting in the Lord with a soft heart so my family will find me approachable and not prickly. Getting to bed at a reasonable time so I can spend quality time in the word and in prayer each morning is essential to being kind and gentle to be around on the morrow. When my family approaches me, I do not want to be continually sighing and telling them I am too tired or this is not a good time. I want to be accessible and approachable, as Jesus always is.

He is gentle, meek, and gives us rest.

"I am gentle and lowly in heart, and you will find rest for your souls." (Matthew 11:29)

Steve is not naturally meek and gentle. Only by

putting on Christ each morning and investing time in His presence will the gentleness and meekness of Jesus rub off on me. I notice Jesus does not act meek and gentle; He is meek and gentle. His gentleness emanates from a gentle spirit and a kind heart. May God help me to embrace meekness and be transformed from the inside out.

He encourages us and does not crush our spirit.
"He will not crush the weakest reed or put out a flickering candle." (Matthew 12:20)

In the book on **Speaking the Truth in Love** I address this topic more fully. God has helped me to be in a better place in my relationship with Him and this new divine connection has spilled over into improving my relationships with my wife and children, I have become aware that when I was in a state of stress or anxiety I could crush my family's spirit with a word or the tone of my voice. This was hard for me to hear. I so want to be an encourager and not a discourager. A builder-upper and not a quencher or crusher. As a husband and father, I want to encourage my family's dreams and aspirations.

Serve one another.
"Jesus called them to him and said, 'You know that the rulers of the Gentiles lord it over them, and their great ones exercise authority over them. It shall not be so among you. But whoever would be great among you must be your servant, and whoever would be first among you must be your slave, even

as the Son of Man came not to be served but to serve, and to give his life as a ransom for many.'" (Matthew 20:25-28)

As a husband, father, and employer, God has given me a certain amount of authority. This authority is not for being the big cheese and lording it over those in my home or business. I want to use my authority for building up those around me. Jesus possessed all divine authority, and He used it for serving and laying down His life.

Addendum

You may get the impression from the the terms, "gentle," "meek," "doesn't crush or quench," "and server," Jesus is not masculine. Nothing could be further from the truth. Meek does not equal weak, but rather it reveals extraordinary inner strength: strength to keep the self under control; strength to prioritize others over self; strength to be diligent and steadfast despite frustrating or oppressive circumstances. Jesus was the embodiment of true masculinity. He had more courage and integrity than anyone who ever lived. He was also safe to be around.

God's Son was a true man and an inspiring leader, and led with the attitude of a servant and not someone who lords it over His followers. I am large (6'5") and can easily be intimidating. I am not naturally meek or gentle. When I hear the word "lead," I am full steam ahead. Taking the lead is second nature to me. I am a type A personality who is a self starter. These passages remind me to find a balance between leading and being gentle; between taking initiative and serving.

Perhaps you are naturally gentle and a server at heart, perhaps God wants to add initiative to your repertoire. I am not trying to push an agenda or define what it means to lead or be masculine. I am hoping we will keep our eyes on Him and trust His Spirit to conform us to His image.

He reveals the Father to us.

"No one knows who the Son is except the Father, or who the Father is except the Son and anyone to whom the Son chooses to reveal him." (Luke 10:22)

Only the Son can sovereignly reveal the Father, and only the Spirit can enable a person to say Jesus is Lord, but I hope to do my part in pointing my sons and grandchildren to God, through my words and deeds.

He seeks us.

"For the Son of Man came to seek and to save the lost." (Luke 19:10)

I know many individuals who do not know God. I mention their names to God in regular prayer, look for opportunities to speak about God, and continue to reach out to them. May God help me to ever be seeking the lost.

**He models the word of God and
is completely consistent.**

"In the beginning was the Word, and the Word
was with God, and the Word was God." (John 1:1)

Jesus was completely consistent. His life perfectly
lined up with the truth. May God help my walk
and talk to be more consistent every day. Life is a
journey and along the way God puts people into our
lives to help us be consistent and not hypocritical.
We all need accountability, but rarely seek it. God
sovereignly gives us several sets of observing eyes
in the form of our spouse and children. As we study
the word together in family worship times, and live
out our faith every day within our home, we each
have the opportunity to help one another apply what
we have read.

He understands our humanity.

"Jesus on his part did not entrust himself to them,
because he knew all people and needed no one to
bear witness about man, for he himself knew what
was in man." (John 2:24–25)

I am human. I make mistakes. I err. I need to
remember not only am I human, so is everyone else
on this planet. There are two ways to apply this verse
for me. One is when others make a mistake, I need
to forgive them and give them a lot of grace. Each
person is fighting the good fight, and I have no idea
what battles they are combatting at the moment.
Only God knows what is going on in every heart.

I also have to remember that I am mortal and

not to be too hard on myself. I have a tendency to beat myself up and achieve unrealistic objectives. I need to find the easy yoke, the light burden, and rest in the Lord. Being too tough on Steve is the work of the "accuser of the brethren" and the "deceiver of the whole world," (Revelation 12:9-10) not our encouraging, meek, and gentle Savior who loves and likes us.

He loved us to the end.

"Now before the Feast of the Passover, when Jesus knew that his hour had come to depart out of this world to the Father, having loved his own who were in the world, he loved them to the end." (John 13:1)

I don't ever want to give up on people. Jesus never did. Regardless of people's behavior, I want to love them to the end as Jesus did. I want to imbibe the spirit of commitment Jesus exemplifies.

He asked His Father to forgive the people who had called for His crucifixion.

"Jesus said, 'Father, forgive them, for they know not what they do.'" (Luke 23:34)

Even when Jesus was hanging on the cross, surrounded by the mob, He continued to love them and ask His Dad to forgive them. This is way out of my bailiwick. If my son was unjustly hanging from the cross, my natural inclination would be to take out those responsible. This is such an incredible display of forgiveness on the part of Jesus. He loved the very people who were crucifying Him.

The purpose of considering these scriptures is to learn from them and then apply them. The first Christian on record to follow the example of Jesus and forgive those who were killing him was Stephen in Acts 7. "They cast him out of the city and stoned him. And the witnesses laid down their garments at the feet of a young man named Saul. And as they were stoning Stephen, he called out, 'Lord Jesus, receive my spirit.' And falling to his knees he cried out with a loud voice, 'Lord, do not hold this sin against them.' And when he had said this, he fell asleep." (Acts 7:58-60)

I couldn't help but notice earlier in the chapter, Stephen, full of the Spirit, had powerfully and fearlessly declared the truth to the Sanhedrin. Jesus had also declared the truth to the religious leaders while full of the Spirit. Stephen was like His master from the way he preached, to the way he forgave.

He embodied the spirit of a foot washer.

"When he had washed their feet and put on his outer garments and resumed his place, he said to them, 'Do you understand what I have done to you? You call me Teacher and Lord, and you are right, for so I am. If I then, your Lord and Teacher, have washed your feet, you also ought to wash one another's feet. For I have given you an example, that you also should do just as I have done to you.'" (John 13:12-15)

Jesus did not seek the chief seats at the banquets, even though He deserved them. He

was the true Lord and Teacher. He had earned His
place as their head. He should have been set apart,
honored, and respected. Instead He washed the feet
of His students. He came to serve, not to be served.

St. Francis possessed and articulated this spirit
of serving, when he prayed, "Grant that I may not
so much seek to be consoled, as to console; to be
understood as to understand, to be loved, as to love."

He loves us as much as He was loved.

"As the Father has loved me, so have I loved
you. Abide in my love." (John 15:9) I am convinced
from my study, to the degree Jesus was loved by
His Father, He was enabled to love us to the same
degree. Since I have grown in my understanding
of how much my Dad loves and likes me, my
corresponding ability to love and like others has
increased. I can only give what I have received. Every
good and perfect gift comes from above. The more
grace I receive, the more grace I am equipped to
give. Perhaps this is why the apostle Peter exhorts
us to, "Grow in the grace and knowledge of our Lord
and Savior Jesus Christ." (2 Peter 3:18)

He gives us the word of God.

"I have given them your word." (John 17:14) By
God's grace and with a bunch of encouragement
from my wife, we have read almost the entire Bible
aloud in our family worship times. It is not my
responsibility to convince or convict, this is the work
of the Spirit. My responsibility is to give them the

word.

Prayer

Thank you Jesus, for being the word made flesh and coming to dwell among us. As we have seen you and your glory, we have seen the Father. You are full of grace and truth. Reproduce your life in us so we may also be the word lived out in our homes, full of grace and truth. In your name we pray, amen. (John 1:14)

QUESTIONS FOR REFLECTION AND STUDY

1. In 1 Timothy 5, how are church relationships tied into family relationships? Explain.
2. What is the difference between ACTING meek and gentle and BEING meek and gentle? (You can also insert other character qualities in place of meek and gentle.)
3. How does it affect you when you grow in understanding of how much your Heavenly Dad loves and likes you?
4. What is meant by "The more grace we receive from God, the more grace we are equipped to give?"
5. Which of these passages resonated with your heart? Why?

CHAPTER 6: TRANSFORMED FROM WITHIN

This book is not meant to be a "how to" manual for how to a better husband or father. Over the years, I have read books and attended seminars on being a better dad and husband. I had heard exhortations to spend more time with my kids, listen to them, pray for each of my sons, and teach them the word of God during family worship times.

As a husband, I have attended workshops and read books where I was exhorted to regularly rekindle our romance, hold hands, observe weekly or monthly date nights, invest time in weekend getaways, pray together, and read the word as a couple. These activities have all proven worthwhile. But I don't ever recall being exhorted to love my wife as I have been loved.

The primary thought or concept of this book is more than new strategies or different approaches to improving family life. Until we are transformed from within our own heart, we can not hope to successfully and effectively love God or others. "Woe to you, scribes and Pharisees, hypocrites! For you clean the outside of the cup and the plate, but inside they are full of greed and self-indulgence. You blind Pharisee! First clean the inside of the cup and the plate, that the outside also may be clean." (Matthew 23:25–26)

Not only are we transformed to love, we are

transformed by loving. The very activity of looking to Jesus, and loving others as we have been loved, conforms and molds us to His image. We are being changed in the endeavor of loving God with all our heart, soul, mind, and strength, and then caring for others as we have been cared for.

There are exhortations for fathers and husbands I need to apply, but who I am will make the most significant impact on what I do. In other words my obedience must flow out of a transformed life to be effective. Jesus did wonderful things and said wonderful words, because Jesus was wonderful from the inside out. Jesus who did not teach anything He was not already living. The reason He could be completely consistent was because He didn't have to act gentle; He was gentle. "I am gentle and lowly in heart." (Matthew 11:29) He didn't have to behave like a shepherd; He was the good shepherd. "I am the good shepherd." (John 10:11)

For us to love as Jesus loved and act as Jesus acted, we have to be changed from the inside out. Transformed relationships begin with transformed hearts. When my heart has been divinely turned to love and know God, then I am in a good place to have God turn my heart to love others in the same form and fashion. As I love God with all my heart, keep my eyes on Jesus, follow His commands from my heart to love them as he loved me, then I will see lasting changes in my family relationships. "I appeal to you therefore, brothers, by the mercies of God, to present your bodies as a living sacrifice, holy and acceptable to God, which is your spiritual worship. Do not be conformed to this world, but be transformed" (Romans 12:1-2)

Jesus was equipped to love others, after He was loved by His Dad. Until I am loved by God, I am not equipped or empowered to love others. Here are some passages which have encouraged me to be a man after God's heart. No one loved God like David (except the Son of David). He was a man after God's heart, who loved God with all his heart, soul, mind, and strength. "The Lord has sought out a man after his own heart, and the Lord has commanded him to be prince over his people." (1 Samuel 13:14)

Even though this next verse is about Solomon, notice what God had to say about David. "When Solomon was old his wives turned away his heart after other gods, and his heart was not wholly true to the Lord his God, as was the heart of David his father." (1 Kings 11:4) David's heart was "'wholly true to the Lord his God."

God knows our heart. He knows the real us. I believe He is the only one who can change and improve our heart. We are powerless to create a revolutionary heart fully devoted to God. But He can. "I will give them a heart to know that I am the Lord, and they shall be my people and I will be their God, for they shall return to me with their whole heart." (Jeremiah 24:7) Let's pray for this inspired work in our hearts regularly and effectually until God changes us from the inside out.

My favorite scripture which shapes how I pray

is found in 1 John 5:14–15. "This is the confidence that we have toward him, that if we ask anything according to his will he hears us. And if we know that he hears us in whatever we ask, we know that we have the requests that we have asked of him." Since the great command is to love God and the new command is to love others as we have been loved, then I believe it is God's will for us to have a heart transplant. For until our heart is changed we are unable to fulfill this good work.

"We are his workmanship, created in Christ Jesus for good works, which God prepared beforehand, that we should walk in them." (Ephesians 2:10)

There is no greater work, nor higher pursuit, than loving God with everything in us and loving others as we have been loved.

Paul himself prays for the believers in Ephesus so they would be supernaturally assisted in this work of loving and being loved. "I do not cease to give thanks for you, remembering you in my prayers, that the God of our Lord Jesus Christ, the Father of glory, may give you the Spirit of wisdom and of revelation in the knowledge of him, having the eyes of your hearts enlightened." (Ephesians 1:16–18)

Loving God and others is heart work. It is created by God and renewed and encouraged by the Spirit of God. Here is another favorite scripture along these same lines. "I will sprinkle clean water on you, and you shall be clean from all your uncleannesses, and from all your idols I will cleanse you. And I will give you a new heart, and a new spirit I will put within you. And I will remove the heart of stone from your flesh and give you a heart of flesh. And I will put my Spirit within you, and cause you to walk in my statutes and be careful to obey my rules." (Ezekiel 36:25-27)

God is the only one who knows what is truly in our heart and recognizes when we are simply going through the motions. I think our spouses and children know us very well also, and quickly discern our heart motivation. I don't think I need to spend time trying to convince anyone of this. These precious folks are closest to us and know us intimately. They know when our walk lines up with our talk. They are quick to spot hypocrisy, when our talk is not consistent with our walk.

Before you get discouraged at this thought of being known by those closest to you, consider that family relationships are an integral part of God's plan to transform and sanctify us. We need each other. We need to be held accountable. Having extra pairs of eyes observing us in our daily conduct not only helps our children learn how to follow Christ, these same eyes motivate us to improve our own walk with God. I keep thinking of this expression, "obedient from the heart." "But thanks be to God, that you who were once slaves of sin have become obedient from the heart to the standard of teaching to which you were committed, and, having been set free from sin, have become slaves of righteousness." (Romans 6:17-18)

When we obey from the heart, where the real us

is hiding, where our true nature is revealed, we are walking in integrity and not in hypocrisy. "Not by the way of eye-service, as people-pleasers, but as bondservants of Christ, doing the will of God from the heart." (Ephesians 6:6) When we love God with all of our heart, our children will know the difference. When we love Jesus, and are seeking to love our spouse as we have been loved, our spouses will sense the difference.

One final thought in this section. Our motivation to love as Jesus loved, cannot be based on a strong desire to be a Godly parent and spouse. The primary impetus to seek God and obey His word, should be the love of Christ, period. It was love for my family that compelled me to search the scriptures and seek to walk in light of Deuteronomy 6. In this chapter, which commands me to teach the word diligently to my children, I discovered the verses which precede this call, direct me to love God and have His word on my heart first. Before I can teach my children to love God and His word, I have to love God and have His word on my heart (Deuteronomy 6:5-7). There are many incentives which God will use to draw us to Himself, but the purest and highest motivation is always the love of God.

Paul writes "For the love of Christ controls us." (2 Corinthians 5:1) The word "controls" may also be rendered "inspires, constrains, impels, or urges." Paul was an exhorter who strove to see believers become more like Jesus. What really drove Him was not His love for the church, but His love for Christ.

"Whatever gain I had, I counted as loss for the sake of Christ. Indeed, I count everything as loss because of the surpassing worth of knowing Christ Jesus my Lord." (Philippians 3:7–8)

Jesus was loved perfectly. He loves us perfectly. This perfect love casts out and banishes all forms of fear (1 John 4:18). The fear of not being accepted, of not belonging, of judgement, of not being in Christ, of not being forgiven. As we assimilate and comprehend the perfect gracious unconditional love of God, we will be motivated and constrained like Paul to have the perfect love of Christ control us!

Prayer

As much as we love our family, our spouse, and the body of believers, help us to love and honor God first and foremost. And may the Lord direct our hearts to the love of God and to the steadfastness of Christ. (2 Thessalonians 3:5)

QUESTIONS FOR REFLECTION AND STUDY

1. 1 John 5:14-15 says that if we ask God for anything according to His will, he will give it to us. Ask God to give you a heart transplant to love God & to love others as He has loved us.

2. Steve shares about various techniques for being a better husband and father that he has heard over the years. While these may be good practices to grow in, for lasting transformation we must be changed from the inside. Can you think of a time you were challenged at an event (e.g. conference or seminar) to change your behavior as a spouse or parent in some way? Think back to what happened next....Can you remember the phases you went through as you tried to change your behavior? What were your thoughts and feelings? Explain.

3. Unpack this statement and discuss it with others: Who I am impacts what I do. Think of examples from Jesus' life on earth that demonstrate this truth and record them here.

4. David was called "a man after God's own heart." What characteristics or behavior showed that?

5. "The primary thought or concept of this book is more than new strategies or different approaches to improving family life. Until we are transformed from within our own heart, we can not hope to successfully and effectively love God or others." Why is this true?

CHAPTER 7:
THE NEW COMMANDMENT IN THE EPISTLES

As wonderful as our study of the gospels has been, the epistles may even be better. I arranged the following scriptures, along with my comments, as they appear in scripture.

He reveals His love by dying for us while we were sinners.

"God shows his love for us in that while we were still sinners, Christ died for us." (Romans 5:8)

This passage illustrates how a verse can speak to us in more than one way. The way this verse speaks to me is: He loved me when I was a weak, unlovable, messy sinner. When I consider the implications of this truth, I am more inclined to love others when they are messy.

I also notice God took the initiative to love me. He didn't wait until I asked to be loved, but died for me when I was blind, messy, and needed Him to take away my sins. The application is not to love those who are compliant and easy to love, but to take the initiative and love those who are not naturally lovable.

He prays for us.

"Christ Jesus is the one who died—more than that, who was raised, who is at the right hand of God, who indeed is interceding for us." (Romans 8:34)

Another similar verse is found in Hebrews 7:25. "Consequently, he is able to save to the uttermost those who draw near to God through him, since he always lives to make intercession for them."

Years ago, I noticed Job offered sacrifices and prayed for His children regularly. "When the days of the feast had run their course, Job would send and consecrate them, and he would rise early in the morning and offer burnt offerings according to the number of them all. For Job said, 'It may be that my children have sinned, and cursed God in their hearts.' Thus Job did continually." (Job 1:5) Because of the example of this Godly father, I began the habit of praying for my children regularly.

The first two passages in this section indicate that after Jesus rose from the dead and ascended to the Father, He is sitting at the right hand of God praying and interceding for you and me. If Jesus is praying, then Steve should be praying. A fringe benefit of praying is as I lift up the needs of others and mention them by name, my heart is inclined to this individual and I believe my love is increased and for them as I do.

Perhaps this is why we are commanded to pray for our enemies and those who persecute us. Perhaps Paul was born from above in answer to the prayers of the early church applying the new commandment, and praying for "those who persecute you." (Matthew 5:44)

Praying for my wife, sons, daughters-in-laws, and grandchildren continually (since Jesus is praying for me) has become a discipline and responsibility God is helping me to do almost every day.

He will let nothing separate us from His love.

"For I am sure that neither death nor life, nor angels nor rulers, nor things present nor things to come, nor powers, nor height nor depth, nor anything else in all creation, will be able to separate us from the love of God in Christ Jesus our Lord." (Romans 8:38–39)

Nothing separates us from God's love, and I am seeking to let nothing keep me from loving my wife and children. Prayer, as we just read, is one way to keep the heart warm towards each other. Remembering birthdays, anniversaries, and communicating with each other aids in this endeavor. May God help us to "keep loving one another earnestly, since love covers a multitude of sins." (1 Peter 4:8)

I don't think we can assume we will always have a natural affinity for one another. I think we need to be intentional and make this a matter of prayer. May God make us like the Thessalonian brethren who were champions of loving one another.

"Now concerning brotherly love you have no need for anyone to write to you, for you yourselves have been taught by God to love one another." (1 Thessalonians 4:9)

He welcomed us.

"Welcome one another as Christ has welcomed

you, for the glory of God." (Romans 15:7)

There are several people in my life who have had warm welcoming smiles. When you visited their homes their faces would light up when they greeted me at the door. My Mom and Dad, my grandparents, my aunt, my pastor, and many other wonderful people possessed a beaming countenance which was always made for a heartwarming welcome.

I believe, based on several inspired verses, God's countenance is beaming when we draw near to Him. Knowing God smiles warmly, I want to always have a warm welcoming facial expression when I greet my wife and children. "The eye is the lamp of the body." (Matthew 6:22) You can't fake a smile. Those who know you well, recognize what is genuine and what is not. I want God to help me love my family so much, a smile naturally radiates from my face as an overflow from the loving heart He is creating in my chest.

He became poor that we might be rich.

"For you know the grace of our Lord Jesus Christ, that though he was rich, yet for your sake he became poor, so that you by his poverty might become rich." (2 Corinthians 8:9)

Perhaps this verse should be included with the others pertaining exclusively to Jesus. Or perhaps children are expensive. Sometimes they make us feel poor. Jesus had everything and yet chose to give it all up to better our condition. So we are called to lay our lives down, take up our cross daily, and put the needs of others ahead of our own. Having small, delicate, needy, dependent babies, brings forth compassion and a desire to help and nurture our children. When our natural desire fades, we look to the great example, and continue to put the needs of others ahead of our own by denying ourselves for our family.

He has washed us with the word.

"He might sanctify her, having cleansed her by the washing of water with the word." (Ephesians 5:26)

My first thought when I read this passage is to read the word of God to, and with, my family. The first non-math related book I wrote was *Family Worship*. Here is a selection from page 24 relating to the benefit of reading the word of God in your home.

After we pray, we take turns reading aloud around the room. Once our boys were able to read for themselves, I purchased large print Bibles, in the same version, so we could all read from the same translation.

We focused on one chapter per day. My reasoning for reading aloud is found in two places in Scripture: "Until I come, devote yourself to the public reading of Scripture, to exhortation, to teaching." (1 Timothy 4:13) "Blessed is the one who reads aloud the words of this prophecy, and blessed are those who hear, and who keep what is written in it, for the time is near." (Revelation 1:3)

Reading, as well as hearing, makes learning more effective. We found that even when we didn't comprehend every verse we read with our minds, our spirits were still being cleansed and nurtured. "Already you are clean because of the word that I have spoken to you." (John 15:3)

He emptied Himself and became a servant.
"Have this mind among yourselves, which is yours in Christ Jesus. Though he was in the form of God, did not count equality with God a thing to be grasped, but emptied himself, by taking the form of a servant, being born in the likeness of men." (Philippians 2:5-7)

I have already mentioned several times how the new command flows from our heart. But in his letter to the church at Philippi, the Apostle Paul encourages us to have the same mind Jesus does. In another one of Paul's epistles, we understand by faith, we already "have the mind of Christ" (1 Corinthians 2:16). This mindset we share with Christ, infiltrates our consciousness until we are willing to let go of what we consider our assets and take the form of a servant.

A good servant is empathetic and able to connect with those he serves. He is tuned into their needs. While I can sense some needs of my family, I am also learning I can be intentional and doing better by asking questions. Some questions I have found to be helpful to open the door to these conversations are: "How are you feeling? How can I help? Is there anything I can pray for you today?" Taking advantage of the tools of social media. Our family has created a private group, not privy to the world of our "friends", where we share announcements and prayer requests.

Perhaps the act of emptying himself enabled Jesus to connect quickly and deeply with people that He encountered. Since He forsook His own agenda, He was able to discern what was important to others. He met the woman at the well and within minutes she was pouring out her life story. He was good friends with Lazarus and his sisters Mary and Martha. He was aware of what His disciples were thinking and feeling. I am not sure if this was His divinity or just His ability to serve and connect with those who were closest to Him. God help me to empty myself and serve my family well.

He forgives us.

"Bearing with one another and, if one has a complaint against another, forgiving each other; as the Lord has forgiven you, so you also must forgive." (Colossians 3:13)

Forgiveness is never easy, but we have no other option. When we are wounded, our natural inclination is to hurt as we were hurt. We desire justice and an eye for an eye. Is this how God loves us? God doesn't give us what we deserve, or we would all be dead. I had the opportunity to attend Bible studies with Dr. R.C. Sproul in my early days as a believer. On one occasion he said something to the effect, "Don't ever pray for justice, you might get it!" I never forgot those words.

Ever since our Adam and Eve ate the forbidden

fruit and weren't eliminated immediately, we have been living in an age of grace and mercy. God is merciful. When Jesus hung on the cross, mercy and truth met, as our sins which demanded death, were laid on him, and we were given life at His expense.

Remembering how God in Christ, has forgiven us, equips us to love others the same way. If we still struggle with forgiving others, perhaps this portion of the Sermon on the Mount will help you. "For if you forgive others their trespasses, your heavenly Father will also forgive you, but if you do not forgive others their trespasses, neither will your Father forgive your trespasses." (Matthew 6:14–15)

He understands our temptation.

"We do not have a high priest who is unable to sympathize with our weaknesses, but one who in every respect has been tempted as we are, yet without sin." (Hebrews 4:15)

Other translations of this verse say Jesus was tempted in "all points" as we were. He tasted each and every temptation we have experienced. Knowing Jesus took on flesh and was born in the likeness of men is comforting and encouraging.

I have often wondered how many kinds of temptation there are. Are there just a few general ones covering all the bases, or is there a plethora of different ones? I think of the most perceptive and encouraging verses addressing temptation. "No temptation has overtaken you that is not common to man. God is faithful, and he will not let you be tempted beyond your ability, but with the temptation He will also provide the way of escape, that you may be able to endure it." (1 Corinthians 10:13)

The New Living Translation (NLT) presents the beginning of this passage a little differently, and makes the point more clear: "The temptations in your life are no different from what others experience." (1 Corinthians 10:13) Each of us experiences the same temptations, as did Jesus.

This helps me relate to my family by recognizing we are all in the same boat. We all seek to overcome similar temptations. This awareness fosters a spirit of compassion and understanding.

He never leaves or forsakes us.

"I will never leave you nor forsake you." (Hebrews 13:5)

My father passed away when I was 47. He never wanted to linger on life support, and while his death was sudden, it was merciful as well. I still miss him. He lived two hundred miles away from us, and knowing he was there was a comfort. I didn't call him every day, but I knew if I did, he would be there for me. And if he could help in any way, he would. He was my dad. He left a fine legacy for my brother and myself.

Jesus is always there for us. In a similar way, want to be present for my wife and sons. I hope they know I will be there for them when they need me, and if there is any way I can help, I will.

He has our back.

"The Lord is my helper; I will not fear; what can man do to me?" (Hebrews 13:6)

There is a new expression which communicates the spirit of constant support and continual care. We tell those who are dear to us, "I have your back." Regardless of what happens, we will be there for them. Jesus has our back. He is our 24/7 helper. With Jesus at our side, we will not fear, regardless of what man can do. God is on our team. David had the same assurance. "The LORD is my rock and my fortress and my deliverer, my God, my rock, in whom I take refuge, my shield, and the horn of my salvation, my stronghold." (Psalms 18:2)

With God as our helper, we are called to have each other's back. "Bear one another's burdens, and so fulfill the law of Christ." (Galatians 6:2) This is what families do. We bear each other's burdens and help each other. It is not our job to fix each other, or solve each other's problems. We are called to be present, to bear, and be with each other through difficult experiences. "If one member suffers, all suffer together;" (1 Corinthians 12:26)

He loves us.

"Beloved, if God so loved us, we also ought to love one another." (1 John 4:11)

It is fascinating how John relates our love for our brothers to our love for God. "If anyone says, 'I love God,' and hates his brother, he is a liar; for he who does not love his brother whom he has seen cannot love God whom he has not seen. And this commandment we have from him: whoever loves God must also love his brother." (1 John 4:20–21)

This verse succinctly states since God loves us we ought to also love each other. I have not found a pithy phrase to communicate this concept, but here is the best I can do so far. To the degree I am loved by God, to a similar degree I am empowered to love others. There seems to be a relationship between my capacity to love others and how much I have assimilated God's care and affection for me. Jesus loved the best. Jesus was also loved the most. His Father loved Him perfectly and completely. He loved us the same way. "As the Father has loved me, so have I loved you." (John 15:9)

In Luke 7 we find the story of a woman who bathed Jesus' feet with her tears, and then anointed them with a costly ointment/perfume/oil. Then he adds, "Therefore I tell you, her sins, which are many, are forgiven—for she loved much. But he who is forgiven little, loves little." (Luke 7:47) There is a correlation between the degree that we are forgiven and how much we love. I believe the same holds true for grace. The more we receive, the more we can give. For we can only give what we have been given.

He first loved us.

"We love because he first loved us." (1 John 4:19)

Our ability to love God and others awakened when we were first loved by our God. We were dead in our sins, without God and without hope. He took the first step towards us and kindled a flame in our hearts. May God help us to love the unlovely among us, love our enemies, and pray for those who persecute us. Our natural tendency is to spend time with those who like us and who we like in return. But God loved us when we were not attractive, and when we did not respond kindly when He sent His son. But "love never fails." (1 Corinthians 13:8 NASB) Even when we don't see the immediate fruit in caring for others, love will emerge victorious in the end.

I hope I never stop loving or let my heart grow cold based on the response of people. God never gives up, and with His help I won't either.

He was faithful.

"Consider Jesus, the apostle and high priest of our confession, who was faithful to him who appointed him" (Hebrews 3:1-2)

This concept has been addressed in other verses, but it is an excellent one to restate. Jesus never changes. He promises to never leave nor forsake us. Jesus is committed to us. Jesus loved us even when we rejected Him. He came to redeem us and He is coming back for us. He was faithful unto death.

I used to have lofty spiritual ambitions to extend the kingdom and bear fruit for God. I wanted to be successful in the kingdom of God. I now find myself praying to simply be faithful, like my savior. Faithful to God. Faithful to the truth. Faithful to my family. Faithful to the body of Christ.

"Christ is faithful over God's house as a son."

(Hebrews 3:6)

He is for us.

After I completed the first draft of this book, I did a search on the computer and discovered the phrase 'for us' is mentioned over thirty times. This single truth has been one of the most significant truths I have compassed in the past few years. My Dad likes me. He is for me. He has my back. He is on my team. I am His adopted son. My name has been changed permanently. I am no longer Steve Demme, but Steve D. God, for I am a part of His family, permanently, and forever.

David understood this verity. "This I know, that God is for me." (Psalms 56:9) So did Paul. "If God is for us, who can be against us?" (Romans 8:31) Now we do too. May God write this divine affirmation on the tablets of our heart.

God is on our team

GIFU is from a Building Faith Families monthly email newsletter. I hope you enjoy it as it expresses the sentiment of these passages.

GIFU

An acronym is an abbreviation often formed from the first letters in a phrase. Some of the more popular ones are ASAP, FYI, LOL, and BTW. As Soon As Possible, For Your Information, Laugh Out Loud, and By The Way. Acronyms are more popular than ever, due to the increase in texting and messaging.

I am proposing we create a new one today. GIFU. I have found this expression in scripture and believe it to be one of the predominant themes in the bible, and one of the most contested.

Elisha understood GIFU. "When the servant of the man of God rose early in the morning and went out, behold, an army with horses and chariots was all around the city. And the servant said, 'Alas, my master! What shall we do?' He said, 'Do not be afraid, for those who are with us are more than those who are with them.' Then Elisha prayed and said, 'O LORD, please open his eyes that he may see.' So the LORD opened the eyes of the young man, and he saw, and behold, the mountain was full of horses and chariots of fire all around Elisha." (2 Kings 6:15–17)

Jesus never doubted that GIFU. "Do you think that I cannot appeal to my Father, and he will at once send me more than twelve legions of angels?" (Matthew 26:53)

David the worshiping, warrior, king knew GIFU "He will command his angels concerning you to guard you in all your ways." (Psalms 91:11) "How precious to me are your thoughts, O God! How vast is the sum of them!" (Psalms 139:17)

Paul was absolutely convinced GIFU. "God shows his love for us in that while we were still sinners, Christ died for us." (Romans 5:8)

John knew GIFU "Little children, you are from God and have overcome them, for he who is in you is greater than he who is in the world." (1 John 4:4)

Have you figured out what phrase is represented

by this abbreviation? The words are found in this passage. "What then shall we say to these things? If God is for us, who can be against us?" (Romans 8:31) "Who is to condemn? Christ Jesus is the one who died—more than that, who was raised— who is at the right hand of God, who indeed is interceding for us." (Romans 8:34)

GIFU, GOD IS FOR US. God is on our team. He loves us to pieces. He has our back, and our front. Nothing can separate us from His love. Amen.

"What then shall we say to these things? If God is for us, who can be against us? He who did not spare his own Son but gave him up for us all, how will he not also with him graciously give us all things?" (Romans 8:31-32)

Have a wonderful day marinating in the eternal truth that God is for us and GOD IS FOR YOU,   .
Steve

Prayer

"If God is for us, who can be against us? He who did not spare his own Son but gave him up for us all, how will he not also with him graciously give us all things? Who shall bring any charge against God's elect? It is God who justifies. Who is to condemn? Christ Jesus is the one who died—more than that, who was raised— who is at the right hand of God, who indeed is interceding for us.

For I am sure that neither death nor life, nor angels nor rulers, nor things present nor things to come, nor powers, nor height nor depth, nor anything else in all creation, will be able to separate us from the love of God in Christ Jesus our Lord." (Romans 8:31-34, 38-39) Thank you.

QUESTIONS FOR REFLECTION AND STUDY

1. God takes the initiative to love us while were sinners. What ways can you take the initiative to love your wife or children?

2. Can you think of anyone in your life whose face lights up when they see you? Write about that and how it makes you feel. Do you light up your face when you see your spouse/kids?

3. Do you have the opportunity to read the Word aloud with your family? If not, consider ways that you could, and try it.

4. Consider the quote: "It's not our job to fix each other or solve each other's problems." How can you bear the burdens your spouse and children are carrying?

5. May God help me to love the unlovely, love my enemy, and pray for those who persecute me. Can you name a person in each of these categories?

CHAPTER 8:
WALK IN THE SPIRIT

The objective of this book is to get our eyes on Jesus and love others as Jesus has loved us. To follow in his footsteps we need to partake of the same heavenly resources He was given, which includes the presence and power of the Good Holy Spirit.

Jesus came to earth on a mission. In order to fulfill His calling, He needed to be filled with the Spirit. Jesus Christ, or Jesus, the Christ, means Jesus, the Anointed. He was anointed by the Holy Spirit, fulfilling and referencing Isaiah 61:1, "The Spirit of the Lord is upon me, because he has anointed me to proclaim good news to the poor. He has sent me to proclaim liberty to the captives and recovering of sight to the blind, to set at liberty those who are oppressed." (Luke 4:18)

He was empowered, equipped, and set apart by the Spirit of God. Knowing we would be unable to love as He loved, or live as He lived, without access to the same Spirit, He spoke of the Spirit before He ascended into heaven. His last instruction to the disciples was for them to tarry until they received the Spirit. Just as Jesus depended on the Spirit, so must we.

At this point I feel the need to write an entire book about the Spirit to do this topic justice, but will try and summarize a few key points which have helped me in my walk. I believe to the degree I sow to the Spirit, walk in the Spirit, cultivate the fruit of the Spirit, and am led by the Spirit, to the same degree I am divinely enabled to love as Jesus loved.

A Friend who Sticks Closer than a Brother

As the earthly ministry of Jesus was drawing to a close, He taught the disciples about the Spirit. "I will ask the Father, and he will give you another Helper, to be with you forever." (John 14:16) "Nevertheless, I tell you the truth: it is to your advantage that I go away, for if I do not go away, the Helper will not come to you. But if I go, I will send him to you." (John 16:7)

The same Spirit who filled, anointed, led, and accompanied Jesus throughout His ministry has been sent to be with us, forever. The word "Helper" in the two preceding verses may also be translated, "Comforter, Intercessor, Advocate, and Strengthener."

With Jesus has our example, we too need to be equipped by the Spirit for the important work of loving members of our family as Jesus has loved us. One of the central passages of Scripture devoted to marriage and family life is found at the end of Ephesians 5 and the beginning of Ephesians 6. These verses are replete with vibrant and helpful commands. However before seeking to apply them in our home, we need to first obey Ephesians 5:18, where we find our hope and secret for success, "Be filled with the Spirit."

I can not naturally lay my life down for my wife, or love her as Christ loved the church, without the power of the Spirit impelling and equipping me day

by day. Thank God for the timely and well-placed
exhortation to be filled with the Spirit!!

Sowing to the Spirit

I am learning to intentionally seek and sow to
the Spirit. "Do not be deceived: God is not mocked,
for whatever one sows, that will he also reap. For
the one who sows to his own flesh will from the
flesh reap corruption, but the one who sows to
the Spirit will from the Spirit reap eternal life."
(Galatians 6:7-8)

One of the ways I seek and sow to the Spirit is to
acknowledge His distinct personhood. The Spirit is
a person and not a force. He has a will, a mind, and
loves. The following verses show us how the Spirit
has His own will, His own mind with thoughts and
purposes, and His capacity to love.

"All these are empowered by one and the same
Spirit, who apportions to each one individually as he
wills." (1 Corinthians 12:11)

"He who searches hearts knows what is the mind
of the Spirit, because the Spirit intercedes for the
saints according to the will of God." (Romans 8:27)

"I appeal to you, brothers, by our Lord Jesus
Christ and by the love of the Spirit." (Romans 15:30)

To experience the fellowship of the Spirit, I have
set aside time to commune, be still, and spend time
with Him. "The grace of the Lord Jesus Christ and the
love of God and the fellowship(communion) of the
Holy Spirit be with you all." (2 Corinthians 13:14)

I also read the book He inspired. "For no

prophecy was ever produced by the will of man, but men spoke from God as they were carried along by the Holy Spirit." (2 Peter 1:21)

Reading the inspired word helps set my mind on the Spirit. "For the mind set on the flesh is death, but the mind set on the Spirit is life and peace," (Romans 8:6).

Walk by the Spirit

"An old man told his grandson, 'My son there is a battle between two wolves inside us all. One is Evil. It is anger, jealousy, greed, resentment, inferiority, lies, and ego. The other is Good. It is joy, peace, love, hope, humility, kindness, empathy, and truth.' The grandson thought about it for a minute and then asked his grandfather: 'Which wolf wins?' The old man quietly replied, 'The one you feed.'"

Sowing to the Spirit, and walking by the Spirit are both excellent offensive strategies to feed the good wolf as the old man mentioned. Instead of seeking to not walk in the flesh, I prefer to make plans to walk in the Spirit, thus nullifying the power of my carnal nature. There is no one way to learn to walk in the Spirit. Some days I consciously ask God to help me keep step with the Spirit. Other days, I ask for a fresh filling of the Spirit. Sometimes I meditate on the fruit of the Spirit. Developing a relationship with the third person of the Trinity is a wonderful opportunity to grow and learn about the character of this quiet member of the Godhead who seems to be in the background.

"Walk by the Spirit, and you will not carry out the desire of the flesh. For the desires of the flesh are against the Spirit, and the desires of the Spirit are against the flesh, for these are opposed to each other, to keep you from doing the things you want to do." (Galatians 5:16-17)

"There is therefore now no condemnation for those who are in Christ Jesus. For the law of the Spirit of life has set you free in Christ Jesus from the law of sin and death. ... in order that the righteous requirement of the law might be fulfilled in us, who walk not according to the flesh but according to the Spirit." (Romans 8:1-2, 4) "If we live by the Spirit, let us also keep in step with the Spirit." (Galatians 5:25)

Cultivate the Fruit of the Spirit.

I have heard a good deal of teaching and many sermons on the fruit of the Spirit. Perhaps this is the reason words describing this fruit have lost some of their meaning to me. I have been helped by consulting *The Message*, which renders them with different verbiage, thus helping me grasp their meaning in a fresh new way. As an example, note the first fruit of the Spirit which is love. *The Message* presents love as affection for others. Here are the nine kinds of fruit with which we are most familiar, followed by *The Message* rendition.

1. Love – affection for others
2. Joy – exuberance about life
3. Peace – serenity
4. Patience – a willingness to stick with things

5. Kindness – a sense of compassion in the heart
6. Goodness – a conviction that holiness permeates people and things
7. Faithfulness – involved in loyal commitments
8. Gentleness – not needing to force our way in life
9. Self-control – able to marshal and direct our energies wisely

As I read through this list, I read them as Jesus has affection for others, Jesus is exuberant about life, and Jesus possesses serenity. For God's son was certainly filled with the Spirit and perfectly exemplified each fruit. I could preach a short sermon on each of these attributes of our savior. I hope these definitions will help you see Jesus in a new way.

Be Led by the Spirit

God leads us all differently. He knows each of our unique personalities and is cognizant of the best way to communicate with each of His children. Sometimes the Spirit has spoken to my spirit, not in an audible voice, but words were used. On other occasions a scripture will be quickened as I read it or hear it quoted in a song or sermon. I am sure there are many times God has led me without a specific word being spoken, but with a calm assurance and peace He is leading and in control.

I just began reading my Bible through again, beginning on January 1 in Genesis and Matthew. I am amazed how many times God spoke to Noah,

Abraham, Isaac, and Jacob, and when reading in Matthew, to Joseph and Mary. God is alive. He desires a vital personal connection with each of us. He will communicate with us as we seek Him and are open to Him. May God give us ears to hear what the Spirit is saying to us today.

"He who has an ear, let him hear what the Spirit says to the churches." (Revelation 2 and 3)

"Jesus, full of the Holy Spirit, returned from the Jordan and was led by the Spirit in the wilderness." (Luke 4:1)

"You gave your good Spirit to instruct them." (Nehemiah 9:20)

Prayer

"Teach me to do your will, for you are my God! Let your good Spirit lead me on level ground!" (Psalms 143:10) Amen.

QUESTIONS FOR REFLECTION AND STUDY

1. Who did Jesus depend on during his life and ministry here on earth? Write a couple of verses that make this clear.

2. Which attribute(s) of the Spirit were new to you?

3. The one who sows to the Spirit will from the Spirit reap eternal life. (Galatians 6:8) What does it mean for us to sow to the Spirit? What are some other phrases in the Bible about what we do with the Spirit?

4. Read over the fruit of the Spirit from The Message, thinking about each one as Jesus lived it while on earth. For example, Jesus has affection for others. Think about and write down examples from the Gospels illustrating each fruit in Jesus' life.

5. Recall times in your life when God has clearly communicated to you. Write about them. Share them with others studying this book with you. They overcame by the blood of the Lamb and the word of their testimony (Revelation 12:11). Your testimony is powerful and encouraging!

CHAPTER 9:
DYING TO LIVE

As a man, I believe I was designed to be a husband and father. Being formed in the image of God, I was divinely formed to die and lay my life down for a worthy cause, just like my savior and master. There is no more worthy cause than loving my wife and children as Christ loved me. When I lay my life down, take up my cross daily, and deny myself, then I die. The good news is that in the process of dying, I find my life. Jesus said, "Whoever would save his life will lose it, but whoever loses his life for my sake will save it." (Luke 9:24)

We know Jesus died to bring life. He laid His life down so we might live. He was born to die. In the same way, men are created to lay down their lives for their family. Women are called to submit, children are called to honor and obey, men are called to die.

It is easy to write and talk about dying, but when I am in the crucible of real life I feel like Wilbur the pig in Charlotte's Web when he finds out he is the source of bacon on the farm. "I don't want to die," he wails. No one does. God brought me through a series of very difficult experiences in 2011 and 2012. I squirmed, I finagled, I offered to make sacrifices, I made threats, and issued ultimatums, all to avoid dying. I documented this journey in Crisis to Christ.

The good Spirit helped me to finally let go and die. I say the Spirit helped me because of this hidden gem "how much more will the blood of Christ, who through the eternal Spirit offered himself without blemish to God, purify our conscience from dead works to serve the living God." Hebrews 9:14 Notice this phrase, "Christ, who through the eternal Spirit offered himself." The eternal Spirit helped Jesus to utter those words which cost Him His life, "nevertheless, not as I will, but as you will" (Matthew 26:39) in the garden of Gethsemane. The same Spirit can help us to deny ourselves daily, as Jesus did, and find life, as Jesus promised.

He then adds these pointed words which seem especially applicable to men, "For what does it profit a man if he gains the whole world and loses or forfeits himself?" (Luke 9:25) Much of our motivation as men is to achieve a level of significance and importance. But this verse restores our eternal perspective. Are we so focused on making a million dollars and gaining the whole world, that we do not see we may be in danger of losing our own life and the life of our family?

Armed with these truths, let us have the same spirit of God's Son we considered in a previous chapter. "Have this mind among yourselves, which is yours in Christ Jesus, though he was in the form of God, did not count equality with God a thing to be grasped, but emptied himself, by taking the form of a servant." (Philippians 2:5-7) May God turn our hearts, in a fresh and powerful way, towards God and our family.

Serve

As a husband I am commanded to love my wife

as Christ loved the church, or as Christ loved me.
This verse is clearly a restating of the new command
where I am called to love my wife as I have been
loved. By meditating on how Jesus has loved me, I
am helped to know how to love my wife.

Jesus taught his disciples they were not to rule
over each other, but serve one other. "You know
that the rulers of the Gentiles lord it over them, and
their great ones exercise authority over them. It
shall not be so among you. But whoever would be
great among you must be your servant, and whoever
would be first among you must be your slave, even
as the Son of Man came not to be served but to
serve, and to give his life as a ransom for many.'"
(Matthew 20:25–28)

Jesus was prompted to teach this concept after
the mother of two of His disciples had just made
an appeal to Jesus to appoint her boys as his chief
lieutenants. The other disciples were upset perhaps
because they wanted these positions for themselves.
Men understand this passage. It is built into a man
to win and be first. Competition is a part of our DNA.
I know the desire to win is not exclusively a man
thing, but it does seem to occupy a large part of our
motivation in life. I don't think I need to belabor this
point; we all are aware of our propensity to be first.

God made men. He knows what makes them
tick. He is aware they are looking for the formula
to be the best disciple. Instead of rebuking or
discouraging this inner drive, He simply explains
how to be number one in His kingdom. Whoever is

the best servant wins! If you want to be first, then be slave to the others. "whoever would be first among you must be your slave" (Matthew 20:27). If I want to be a great husband and father, God shows me how. Follow the Son of Man, who "came not to be served but to serve."

This kind of thinking and teaching is counterintuitive and God knows it will take time for people grasp this concept which is foreign to them. So He follows the teaching with an illustration. "When He had washed their feet and put on his outer garments and resumed his place, He said to them, 'Do you understand what I have done to you? You call me Teacher and Lord, and you are right, for so I am. If I then, your Lord and Teacher, have washed your feet, you also ought to wash one another's feet. For I have given you an example, that you also should do just as I have done to you.'" (John 13:12–15)

Washing feet is a humbling act. As a husband, my role is not to be the king of my castle. My wife and children were not created to serve me. I have been designed to serve them. By meditating on how Jesus loved me by serving me and washing my feet, I follow His example and do not treat my wife and children as second class citizens, but as fellow children of God, who were also created in the image of God.

Washing

This past year I was thinking of how I could serve my wife. The kitchen was in need of some attention so I washed the dishes in the sink, emptied and loaded the dishwasher, and took out the trash. I was hoping for a surprised smile, and an appreciative thank you. When she arrived home, I expectantly awaited the recognition, but it never came. While she is usually very quick to thank me, she didn't say a word.

Instead of pouting or quietly drawing her attention to what I had done, I thought of how many times Jesus had done things for me which went unrecognized and without my thanking Him, yet he continued to do them anyway. So I let it go. This is new territory for me. When I do something special, I want to be acknowledged. I want a parade or at least a medal. Then I thought of the thousands of times she had made that kitchen sparkle and I had never thanked her. Jesus came to serve, so can I.

Ask

I don't recall the particulars of a conversation Sandi and I had, but during our discussion I learned I have been guilty of treating her like a second class citizen. When I learned she felt this way, I sincerely apologized, and have sought in many and varied ways to serve her, build her up, and esteem her highly.

One practical way I have sought to treat her with respect and dignity is not correcting her when she is recounting an incident in the life of our family. Whether it is an amusing anecdote or how she recalled the events which led up to our own engagement and marriage, I let her finish without interrupting. I often remember the sequence of events a little differently, but I am learning to smile and let it go.

One way to find out how to serve your wife is to ask her. For example, I have recently discovered how much work it is for Sandi to put together a special occasion for our family, like a birthday celebration or a holiday. She likes to cook and set a beautiful table, but it takes a lot of energy and time, and she is tired after the meal. I am now the official cleaner-upper after these events and oversee the washing of the dishes and the storing of the leftovers, while she enjoys her family. I had a good example set for me; my dad would do this for my mom. But it took my thirty plus years into my marriage before I followed suit! With God helping me to have the heart of a servant, I am enjoying practical ways to build up, encourage, and serve my family.

One more tip, make sure you are earnest in your desire to serve and not just looking for a quick and easy way to do some good or get out of the doghouse. If you are not all-in and totally committed to her welfare and she does not feel your heart, then she will not be completely open to you. Give her time. And be persistent.

Back to how I treated Sandi. Jesus could have treated each of us like second class citizens, for compared to Him, we are. But he chose a different path. "Though he was in the form of God, did not count equality with God a thing to be

grasped, but emptied himself, by taking the form
of a servant, being born in the likeness of men."
(Philippians 2:6-7) These verses, which I think of
often, follow the third verse which says we are
to "do nothing from selfish ambition or conceit,
but in humility count others more significant than
yourselves." I am not the first class citizen in the
home. I am not above my wife. We are joint-heirs
and both valued members of the body of Christ. We
each have something to offer the church. This is not
to say we have the same roles or responsibilities, but
we are one in Christ Jesus and both adopted children
of God. I may have been called to be the head of the
home, but Jesus is the head of the church and he
took the form of a servant.

Submit

"Wives, submit to your own husbands, as to the
Lord. For the husband is the head of the wife even
as Christ is the head of the church, his body, and
is himself its Savior. Now as the church submits to
Christ, so also wives should submit in everything to
their husbands." (Ephesians 5:22-24)

As I have mentioned in an earlier section, wives
are called to submit, this is clear. But it is not for me
to see she does.

I like to think of the command for my wife to
submit, as found in a letter addressed to her. It
is not my job to read her mail, or to see that she
applies this scripture. That is her responsibility. My
job is to serve her and deny myself. Whether she

decides to submit or not is between her and her heavenly King. My responsibility is not to fix, but to love as Jesus loved. "Husbands, love your wives, as Christ loved the church and gave himself up for her." (Ephesians 5:25)

Most married couples have had some teaching on submission and could quote verses of Ephesians 5:22–24. It is helpful to note this section follows Ephesians 5:21, "submitting to one another out of reverence for Christ." Submission is not only for the ladies but for the men as well. Both of us are to submit to one another "out of reverence to Christ" who is Lord of both the husband and the wife. "All scripture is inspired and profitable" (2 Timothy 3:16), not just our favorite portions.

Faithful

Jesus is committed to marrying His bride. His love for us began before we were born and He has never swerved from His intent to marry us. "Let us rejoice and exult and give him the glory, for the marriage of the Lamb has come, and his Bride has made herself ready." (Revelation 19:7)

This passage is also found in the section on ways Jesus exclusively loves us on page 49. Only He will marry us. We can learn from His eternal commitment to us to be faithful to one another while on this earth.

We know "he chose us in him before the foundation of the world." (Ephesians 1:4) God has had the marriage of His Son on His heart before the

world was created. Jesus never wavered from this
commitment. He came to redeem us from sin which
separates us from God so we might be eternally
united. "I go and prepare a place for you, I will come
again and will take you to myself, that where I am
you may be also." (John 14:3) I have been told this
language is descriptive of a first century Jewish man,
who would prepare a place for His bride and then
come back for her.

The application is evident. May God help us to
be committed to our spouses, just as Jesus was
committed to His bride. He never altered His course
even when we were wayward and adulterous, He
remained steadfast in His affection and His intent to
wed us.

Prayer

"May the God of peace who brought again from
the dead our Lord Jesus, the great shepherd of the
sheep, by the blood of the eternal covenant, equip
you with everything good that you may do his will,
working in us that which is pleasing in his sight,
through Jesus Christ, to whom be glory forever and
ever. Amen." (Hebrews 13:20–21)

If you would like to learn more about how
God has led me to love my wife based on the New
Commandment, consider listening to these podcasts.
Transcriptions are also available for those who prefer
to read the content.

218   The Husband's Calling in Marriage, part 1
219   With Authority (Husbands) Comes
        Responsibility, part 2

buildingfaithfamilies.org/podcasts/

QUESTIONS FOR REFLECTION AND STUDY

For men:
1. What were you created for, according to this chapter and God's Word?
2. What does it mean to you that you are the "head" of your household? What did Jesus, as Head of the church, do? (If you are not married, apply this to your sphere of influence, whether your family, church, work, or friends.)
3. What does the Bible say about how you and your wife are BOTH first-class citizens in your home? Do your actions reflect that truth?
4. Find two new ways you can serve your wife. Before you do anything, first check your heart. Are you earnest in your desire to serve her and not just looking for a quick and easy way to "get brownie points" or "get out of the doghouse"? Don't look for gratitude and affirmation; look to Jesus as your example in this quest to serve your wife.

For women:
1. What are you as a wife called to do? (If you are not married, apply these ideas and questions to other relevant relationships.)
2. Pray earnestly for your husband. Choose some verses from this chapter and pray them often, with your husband's name in them. If you want to change your husband, remember only the Holy Spirit can bring conviction.
3. Pray for yourself, that you will be able to submit out of reverence to Christ (Ephesians 5:21).

CHAPTER 10:
FOR PARENTS

I used to wish I was Dr. James Dobson (Christian author, psychologist, and founder of Focus on the Family) or Josh McDowell (Christian minister, expert on youth, and author). I wanted to be like them, full of wisdom and plenty of experience, so I could lead my children well. Then I became a parent, and after years of giving it my best shot, discovered I was a lot like my dad. Some things my dad did I tried to improve upon, others I tried to emulate.

In the west we have a tendency to think of ourselves as individual islands, unaffected by our upbringing. I never consciously thought about my mom and dad and what kind of parents they were. Nor did I reflect on how they were raised. If I copied much of their parenting style, perhaps they were parenting as their parents had raised them.

I have found it very helpful to intentionally think about this topic. Instead of dismissing how I was raised, I found that by asking myself a series of questions helped me to understand them. Now that I am older I also considered how their parents(my grandparents) raised them.

I pulled together a list of questions to help guide your thinking and give you insight into how you were raised. I am discovering that my upbringing impacted my personal development and is presently influencing my relationship with my wife and sons. After working through these questions myself, I was

pleasantly surprised to see how much I was like my
dad and mom. I hope they are as helpful to you as
they were to me.

After you have reflected on how you were raised,
ask yourself how you would like to have been
raised. Ponder what you wish your parents had done
differently. How would you like to have been loved,
disciplined, encouraged, etc.? It is my hope that
working through these questions will set the stage
for many intimate conversations with your spouse,
and increase your understanding of each other, thus
deepening your friendship. I also pray this process of
reflection will reveal some blindspots and enable you
to be a better parent. All of these outcomes will help
you grow as a couple and as a family.

I found it was helpful to keep a journal or record
of what I learned, which I continue to revisit. My
parents have passed on, but if they were alive I
would like to ask them to answer these questions
and hear what they had to say. If your parents are
still living, you may want to set up a time for an
interview after your season of reflection. If you are
seeking more input, it could be profitable to ask
your spouse and children if they see any similarity
between you and your parents. This series of
questions is long, but by no means exhaustive.
For those of you who grew up in blended families,
and were raised by a stepmother, stepfather,
grandparent, or older sibling, then think of them
when thinking through the questions.

Consider your parents

1. Did your parents or caregivers assign specific roles to different genders? For example, fathers are the providers and mothers are the homemakers.
2. Did your parents/caregivers teach you about the birds and the bees? Which parent?
3. How did they express love and affection between themselves?
4. Did they want a large family or small one? Why?
5. How was love shown or expressed to you as a child?
6. Who disciplined the children in your family, and how was it carried out?
7. Did they have healthy relationships with their parents, your grandparents?
8. Did they believe in God, and if so, where did you worship?
9. Did they set aside times for family worship at home? Did they pray before eating?
10. What kind of work ethic was exhibited?
11. Who earned the money? Who decided where it was spent?
12. Who managed the household income and paid the bills?
13. Who did the household chores? Who cut the grass and washed the car?
14. Who bought and prepared the food?
15. How did they celebrate Christmas and Thanksgiving? What parts of your family holiday traditions do you value and hope to maintain?
16. Did they have close friends? How did they

relate to their neighbors?

17. How did they relate to cousins, in-laws, and extended family?

18. What are your favorite family memories growing up?

19. What were the most significant events of your childhood?

20. What were the most significant events of your parents' childhood?

21. What were their views and habits of giving? Did they tithe?

22. What did they think about debt for a house, college, a car, or vacation?

23. How did they decide what kind of car to buy? Did they purchase new or used cars?

24. Did they value college and higher education?

25. How did they define success and a successful life?

26. Did you have a family vacation annually?

27. How did they view recreation and what did they do for fun?

28. How did your parents handle conflict between themselves?

29. How did they view and exhibit anger?

30. How did they communicate with one another?

31. How did they communicate with the children?

32. How did they process grief and loss of a loved one?

33. Do you see any resemblance between yourself and your parents? Where?

34. Do you see areas where you have done the

opposite of what your parent's did?

For extra insight, go through this list and see if you can also answer these questions for your grandparents. This was helpful for me, because after some thought, I realized my Dad's father was not always kind to my Dad. I recognize now my grandfather could be downright mean. I thank God and rise up to honor my father for trying and succeeding in giving me a much better childhood than he experienced. I had harbored some resentment towards my Dad for what he didn't do with and for me, until I discovered what he had endured from his parents. When I worked through this list of questions for grandparents, I developed a much greater admiration for my own parents.

Others have written more on this process, which is sometimes called creating a genogram. A genogram is sort of an expanded family tree, adding a visual representation of the relationships among family members. It can include illnesses, life events, and emotional ties. This graphic makes it easy to recognize and analyze generational patterns. I learned of them in a class I took on Family Systems Theory, and also in the book, Emotionally Healthy Spirituality, by Peter Scazzero.

Soren Kierkegaard observed "life is lived forward but understood backward." Examining my roots has been an enlightening journey in helping me to understand myself. It has also been a freeing experience. As I see myself more objectively, I am able to recognize unhealthy patterns of behavior, and with God's help, change them.

The Ideal Parent Child Relationship

When we complete reflecting on our parents and grandparents, we may have discovered we raise our own children a lot like we were parented. If we had a painful childhood we probably attempt to give our children a happy childhood. Whether we raise our children the same way we were raised, or do the exact opposite, we are deciding how to parent based on our own experience. This is treating our children as we would like to have been treated, which is the royal law we noted in the first chapter. As good as it is, it is horizontal.

Reflecting on the past is helpful, but only a beginning, for the million dollar question is how can we love and raise our children for His glory? God is giving us an alternative in the New Commandment. With this vertical approach, He is lovingly suggesting we parent as He parented. His word, which is given for our good, is calling us to love our children as Jesus has loved each of us, who are His adopted children.

Let's examine the best father–son relationship ever, between God the Father and Jesus the Son. As I seek to love my children and parent them **AS** the Father parented His Son, the best preparation for me is to learn more about their relationship.

Jesus was loved perfectly. I am sure Mary and Joseph were Godly parents, but His Father in heaven was a perfect Dad. "Every good gift and every perfect gift is from above, coming down from the Father of lights with whom there is no variation or shadow due to change." (James 1:17) "God is love." (1 John 4:8) Everything that is good and perfect comes from God, including His love.

Here are some principles for parents I discovered in the Gospels. I will make a few comments about how these passages impact me as a dad to stimulate your own thinking. You will probably have different thoughts of how you can apply these principles with your children. Have fun reading the word of God!

**God the Father affirmed Jesus
the Son at his baptism.**

"When Jesus was baptized, immediately he went up from the water, and behold, the heavens were opened to him, and he saw the Spirit of God descending like a dove and coming to rest on him; and behold, a voice from heaven said, 'This is my beloved Son, with whom I am well pleased.'" (Matthew 3:16–17)

This was a very significant event. It was a graduation and a commencement all in one. He had completed His thirty year training course and was beginning His ministry. His Dad was there. Just as God the Father was present, I too want to be present for important events in the life of my children. Birthdays, graduations, awards ceremonies, weddings, and any other event which is important; I want to be on site and affirm them.

God said, in the hearing of all present, "This is

my boy. And I love him to pieces." There are no more meaningful words for a son to hear than that his dad loves him and he is well pleased with who he is. The Father said simply "I love you for who you are. You are my boy and I couldn't be more thankful."

In that same spirit, I write birthday cards for each of my boys every year. I pray and ask God to help me see them as He sees them, on the inside and not on the outside. I am always amazed at how my perspective changes as He helps me see their character and how they are becoming more like Jesus. These letters are affirmations without a hint of exhortation. This is how God the Father affirmed His Son.

On the Mount of Transfiguration

"He was still speaking when, behold, a bright cloud overshadowed them, and a voice from the cloud said, "This is my beloved Son, with whom I am well pleased; listen to him." (Matthew 17:5)

We are not sure whether this took place on Mt. Tabor or Mt. Hermon, but God uttered a reaffirmation to His Son in the hearing of the disciples. The difference in this utterance is the disciples were told to listen and to pay attention to what Jesus told them. It is always nice to have a father support you in your business or ministry. I bet those fellows paid more attention after hearing divinity speak from a cloud!

His Father always heard Him.

"So they took away the stone. And Jesus lifted up his eyes and said, "Father, I thank you that you have heard me. I knew that you always hear me." (John 11:41– 42)

I am afraid I have dropped the ball on this one. One of my sons did a good bit of talking when he was younger and I began to tune out his frequency. We were at a gathering of people and he was trying to get my attention by saying, "Pop, Papa, Dad, Daddy," and other appellations to no avail. Finally he said, "Mr. Demme," and I looked over to where he was standing, smiling. Sigh. When I read the Father always heard His Son, I am convicted. So I repent, and get back up and listen better!

The Father trusted His Son.

"The Father loves the Son and has given all things into his hand." (John 3:35)

Giving increased responsibility is never easy, but essential to training our children and helping them grow up. Whether driving a car, performing a task, watching their siblings, learning how to hunt, cutting the grass, or washing the dishes, we need to pass the baton to our kids. In doing so, we are trusting them, which makes them know they are loved and trusted.

The Father shows His Son what he is doing.

"Jesus said to them, 'Truly, truly, I say to you, the Son can do nothing of his own accord, but only what he sees the Father doing. For whatever the Father does, that the Son does likewise. For the Father loves the Son and shows him all that he himself is doing. And greater works than these will He show him, so that you may marvel.'" (John 5:19–20)

I think of this verse often in my own life. I want to be about my Father's business and doing what God is doing. I believe God is turning the hearts of families to Him and then toward each other. As a father of sons, I want to communicate to them what I am doing. The best way I can do this is by including them in my business, my ministry, my hobbies, the life of the church, doing chores and repairs around the house, or helping widows and orphans. As I let them see what I are doing, let them hear my conversations, and welcome them watch me interact with others, I am showing my children what I am doing!

The Father taught His Son.

"So Jesus said to them, 'When you have lifted up the Son of Man, then you will know that I am he, and that I do nothing on my own authority, but speak just as the Father taught me.'" (John 8:28)

I have penned a book called ***The Christian Home and Family Worship***, in which I share how God led us to teach the word of God diligently to our sons. Deuteronomy exhorts parents to not only teach the word of God, but also model it, as we walk, sit, lie down, and rise in our homes. Both approaches are a part of our responsibility to teach our children.

Families are also where children learn how to relate to one another. They learn how to love and forgive. I think there should be a book entitled Everything I Needed to Know I Learned at Home.

The Father is with His Son.

"He who sent me is with me. He has not left me alone, for I always do the things that are pleasing to him." (John 8:29)

The firs half of this passage declares the Father was always with the Son. I spoke at a family weekend conference a few months ago. During one of the sessions, where all the children were present, I asked one young fellow what he liked to do best. He said he liked to be with his dad. It didn't matter what his dad was doing, he just liked hanging around him and helping with whatever activity he was engaged in. His remarks were simple, straightforward, and without guile. He liked to be with his dad.

Moses left Egypt and traveled into a forbidding wilderness with over a million people in tow, and one promise. God told him, "I will be with you." (Exodus 3:12) Jesus told his followers, after he commissioned them to make disciples in all the world, "I will be with you always." (Matthew 28:20) His name Immanuel, means "God with us." (Matthew 1:23) We are adopted children of God and nothing is better than knowing we are pleasing, in Christ, and He is with us always.

The second part of this verse affirms Jesus always did what is pleasing to His Father. Children want to do what is pleasing to their parents. I asked a group of families if I could have their kids fill out an anonymous survey about family relationships. All agreed and after the papers were gathered I shared the results with the parents. It was fascinating reading. One item which struck me was the number of kids who did not know what their parents expected of them, and as a result did not know if their parents were ever pleased with them or not. If there are not clearly defined expectations, we will all be living in a state of wondering where we stand and how we are doing.

I boarded at two homes while I was a student in seminary. One home had a one-page typewritten set of expectations. The rules of the home were spelled out very clearly. As a twenty-five year old who had just lived with no rules for four years in college, I was a little offended by this set of laws. The next home had no specified rules, and even though I think they liked having me live in their home, I never really knew. I discovered it was easier to live where there are defined boundaries and expectations.

The Father and Jesus are in unity.
"I and the Father are one." (John 10:30) There is nothing like being on the same team with our children. Family unity is wonderful. Sometimes at a holiday gathering, my wife and I will look at each other and start to cry. Oneness is a gift, which we do not take for granted. "How good and how pleasant it is when brothers dwell together in unity," the

Psalmist proclaims. (Psalm 133:1) When children are younger they accept much of their parents' belief system and convictions. When they get older, and they begin to assert their independence, even the most reverently held belief may be questioned.

I did not always know how to embrace differing opinions within our family. Arguments ensued, and eventually invisible boundaries were established and we all knew what topics were suitable for discussion and which ones were off limits. Trying to work together in a family business led to deep divides and without the help of a counselor, grace, humility, and a commitment to each other, we would be living in different parts of the country. God helped us learn how to value one another, give each other space, and still love and work together even when we have differing convictions. Some of this journey is recounted in Crisis to Christ. Learning how to communicate was a key piece to this puzzle, and the principles we learned and practiced are amplified in Speaking the Truth in Love.

"I therefore, the prisoner in the Lord, beseech you to walk worthily of the calling wherewith ye were called, with all lowliness and meekness, with longsuffering, forbearing one another in love; giving diligence to keep the unity of the Spirit in the bond of peace." (Ephesians 4:1-3 ASV)

The Father Knows the Son

"I am the good shepherd. I know my own and my own know me, just as the Father knows me and I know the Father;" (John 10:14-15)

"No one knows who the Son is except the Father, or who the Father is except the Son and anyone to whom the Son chooses to reveal him." (Luke 10:22)

"O righteous Father, even though the world does not know you, I know you." (John 17:25)

They knew each other, even when no one else did. Knowing my wife and sons and being known by them is a worthy pursuit. My wife and I took a class about Christian Coaching when our sons were in their late teens and early twenties. One of our takeaways was to learn how to ask good questions. I have a responsibility as a dad to teach, train, and give information to my sons. When they become young men, my calling changes to becoming someone who asks good questions, listens well, and helps them make their own decisions. In the process, I have the joy of seeing these incredible young fellows become men. I get to know them in a whole new way and learn so much from them. They all belong to a different church, and while being brothers and having much in common, they are each unique. I just got back from lunch with one of my sons. I asked a lot of questions, and then I shared what was going on in my world. It is lovely to know and be known by those you love and care for.

The Father loved the Son.

"Father ... you loved me before the foundation of the world." (John 17:24)

May God help us to love our children, as God the

Father loved Jesus His only begotten Son. Amen.

Prayer

"May the Lord make you increase and abound
in love for one another and for all, as we do
for you, so that he may establish your hearts
blameless in holiness before our God and Father,
at the coming of our Lord Jesus with all his saints."
(1 Thessalonians 3:12–13)

If you would like to learn more about how
God has led me to love my wife based on the New
Commandment, consider listening to these podcasts.
Podcasts 169–173 Influence of Fathers,
buildingfaithfamilies.org/podcasts/page/6/
Podcasts 204–207 Eternal Principles to Help
Parents Raise Their Children to Live Forever,
buildingfaithfamilies.org/podcasts/page/3/

QUESTIONS FOR REFLECTION AND STUDY

1. This chapter has many built-in reflection questions already. Use the questions listed as a guide to reflection to give you insight into how your upbringing impacted your personal development and is presently influencing your marriage and parenting.

2. After you answer these questions, think about things you wish your parents had done differently. Take as your inspiration Soren Kierkegaard's saying, "Life is lived forward but understood backward."

3. As you read through the scriptures and take a peek at the "best father-son relationship ever," jot notes about whatever verses strike you, and what ways you have successfully applied and can apply these principles in the future to your own interaction with your children. Be as specific and detailed as possible!

4. What provokes and discourages your wife and children?

5. What is your vision for your marriage and family?

6. Do you find that you imitate your earthly parents or your Heavenly Father?

CHAPTER 11: THE NEW COMMANDMENT AND ME

I hesitate to write this chapter, for we live in a narcissistic culture which seems to fulfill this description of the last days. "Understand this, that in the last days there will come times of difficulty. For people will be lovers of self." (2 Timothy 3:1-2) The last thing I want to do is encourage this spirit, but there is a balance to be found between being a lover and worshipper of self, and seeing ourselves as God sees us. I desire to have a heavenly and healthy view of myself as created in the image of God and redeemed for His glory.

Knowing in my heart of hearts God likes me, has helped me to treat myself differently. This is in keeping with the new command to love myself, **AS** God in Christ loves me. I am aware "no one ever hated his own flesh," (Ephesians 5:29) but I did not value myself until I began to grasp the truth that my Heavenly Dad valued me. I am learning to see myself through His eyes instead of my own.

The Father and the Son

As I have pondered how the Father loved His Son, I think one event sums up their relationship. "When Jesus was baptized, immediately he went up from the water, and behold, the heavens were opened to him, and he saw the Spirit of God descending like a dove and coming to rest on him." (Matthew 3:16)

As Jesus emerged from the water, and saw the
Holy Spirit alight on Him, God the Father uttered one
inspired and incredible sentence which is packed
with meaning to His boy, "and behold, a voice from
heaven said, 'This is my beloved Son, with whom
I am well pleased.'" (Matthew 3:17) Or as the NLT
renders the same verse, "This is my dearly loved Son,
who brings me great joy."

I have given much thought to the relationship
between the Father and the Son. One of my biggest
takeaways is that Jesus was a loved Son before He
emerged as a loving Savior. When Jesus embarked
on His short time of ministry, He did so with the
knowledge that God the Father loved Jesus the Son
to pieces.

Before I can hope to be a loving husband and
father, I need to duo whatever it takes to be rooted
and grounded in the knowledge that I am a loved
adopted son of God. I am dearly loved, and I bring
my Dad great joy. For as the Father loves Jesus so
does He like and love us.

Yellow Margarine Container

When I travel, I prefer to fly on Southwest
Airlines. One of the reasons is they have a sense of
humor. As the plane is moving down the runway, the
flight attendants take their positions and give their
spiel about how to buckle, where the exit rows are
located, no smoking in the bathrooms, etc.

On one flight, the person giving the instructions
was explaining what to do if there was a loss of

cabin pressure and the oxygen masks fell from the overhead compartment. The attendant said "When the margarine containers fall, first place the mask on yourself and then help your children."

I have thought about this picture many times. Our first reaction is to make sure our children had access to the flow of oxygen. It is counterintuitive to put on our own mask first, but there is wisdom in what they tell us. For if the parents are not able to breathe, they will not be able to help their children.

The best thing I can do as a husband and father is invest time each morning with the yellow margarine container over my face. This may include reading a few chapters from the Bible, or being still waiting on God, walking with God, or praying for my family. Until I am breathing the divine air and being loved from above, I will not be prepared to love my family.

As I seek God and am refreshed, refilled, and refueled in His presence, I am divinely equipped to be a source of life and comfort to those who are nearest and dearest to me.

For most of my life, I have had trouble taking care of myself and rarely made time to rest, relax, and enjoy life. I felt guilty if I was not engaged in some form of activity which would extend or benefit the kingdom. I recognize I have ascetic tendencies and lean towards a radical Saint Francis lifestyle which might not be helpful. Comprehending that God values me for who I am and not for what I do, gives me permission to embrace a more balanced outlook on life. I am trying to remember it is God who "richly provides us with everything to enjoy." (1 Timothy 6:17)

When I do take care of my body, which is the temple of the Holy Spirit, I am much nicer to be around. By resting, being still, and making time to wait on God, I find I am kinder, gentler, and more loving. I am learning to go to bed earlier, make time to enjoy people and things, and relax. In other words, believing the gospel, is bearing good fruit in my relationship with God and my family.

We each have to seek God and work out our own salvation. What recharges the batteries for one person may drain the life out of another. God is alive and as we seek Him, He will lead us. He is the one who beckons us to, "Come to me, all who labor and are heavy laden, and I will give you rest. Take my yoke upon you, and learn from me, for I am gentle and lowly in heart, and you will find rest for your souls. For my yoke is easy, and my burden is light." (Matthew 11:28–30)

We are each unique and valuable for who we are and not for what we do. There is no one else like us. Everyone is a special blend of a spiritual gift, a personality, a heritage, with an upbringing like no one else. I am learning to be comfortable in my own skin. This includes being grateful for how God made me, who my parents are, and what gift he has given me. God is helping me to give thanks and be content, instead of wishing I was someone else or had a different makeup or gift. "God arranged the members in the body, each one of them, as he chose." (1 Corinthians 12:18)

In the words of Parker Palmer, author, activist, and founder of the Center for Courage & Renewal, "Self care is never a selfish act; it is simply good stewardship of the only gift I have, the gift I was put on earth to offer others. Anytime we can listen to true self and give it the care it requires, we do it not only for ourselves, but for the many others whose lives we touch."

Walking in integrity and being true to ourselves not only benefits those closest to us, it also benefits the greater body of Christ. We each have something special to supply to the church. "As each has received a gift, use it to serve one another, as good stewards of God's varied grace." (1 Peter 4:10) Each of us needs to be and do what God designed us to be and do. If we are all feet or all hands, then the body is not equipped to function as it was designed by God.

"For the body does not consist of one member but of many. If the foot should say, 'Because I am not a hand, I do not belong to the body,' that would not make it any less a part of the body. And if the ear should say, 'Because I am not an eye, I do not belong to the body,' that would not make it any less a part of the body. If the whole body were an eye, where would be the sense of hearing? If the whole body were an ear, where would be the sense of smell? But as it is, God arranged the members in the body, each one of them, as he chose. If all were a single member, where would the body be? As it is, there are many parts, yet one body." (1 Corinthians 12:14–20)

In our churches today, those on the stage, preachers, teachers, and worship leaders, seem to be most admired. They might be the mouth. But we also need the servants behind the scenes to make the body function as it should. We need feet, hands, ears, and each part in the proper proportion.

I have a tendency to emulate others. When I am at a missionary conference, I am ready to sign up and go the ends of the earth. When I listen to believers who live in urban sections of our community, I want to buy a house and serve in this arena. While the spirit of wanting to serve in various places and ministries is admirable, it is better to discover God's design for me and be led by His Spirit. "For we are God's masterpiece. He has created us anew in Christ Jesus, so we can do the good things he planned for us long ago." (Ephesians 2:10)

Rabbi Zusya, as an old man said, "In the coming world, they will not ask me, 'Why were you not Moses?' they will ask me, 'Why were you not Zusya?'" It took me a long time to realize my name is Steve and God has a unique work for me. "Now you are the body of Christ and individually members of it. And God has appointed in the church first apostles, second prophets, third teachers, then miracles, then gifts of healing, helping, administrating, and various kinds of tongues. Are all apostles? Are all prophets? Are all teachers? Do all work miracles? Do all possess gifts of healing? Do all speak with tongues? Do all interpret? But earnestly desire the higher gifts. And I will show you a still more excellent way." (1 Corinthians 12:28–31)

Prayer

"To him who is able to keep you from stumbling and to present you blameless before the presence of his glory with great joy, to the only God, our Savior, through Jesus Christ our Lord, be glory, majesty, dominion, and authority, before all time and now and forever. Amen." (Jude 24–25)

QUESTIONS FOR REFLECTION AND STUDY

1. What is the difference between being a lover and worshipper of yourself, and valuing yourself the way your Heavenly Dad values you? In your thoughts about yourself, do you lean more towards the former or the latter?

2. What insights have you received in recognizing that Jesus was a loved son before becoming a loving Savior?

3. What are some things you do to "recharge"?

4. Who benefits when we take time to care for ourselves and learn to value ourselves the way God does?

5. What is the meaning behind the question Rabbit Zusya proposed near the end of his life, "'In the coming world, they will not ask me, "Why were you not Moses?" They will ask me, "Why were you not Zusya?"'" Explain.

CHAPTER 12: TRANSFORMED IN LOVE

One night, our young family was sitting down to eat at a restaurant. The boys were six, four, and almost two. We had just placed our order and were sitting at the table with nothing to do so I dipped the tip of my finger into my glass of water and flicked it at one of the boys. I thought it was a fun and harmless gesture, but I learned otherwise. Each of them plunged their hands into their water and doused the table and each other with water. My wife sat serenely and didn't say a word. She just looked at me and raised her eyebrow as if to say, "You started this not me."

We all need accountability, especially men. So God gives us several pairs of eyes to watch what we do. These are not peers we meet with for breakfast once a week or twice a month for an hour. These special people are on the job during all of their waking hours. They are called children and live in our home. They pick up our mannerisms and show us how we look. Blind spots are brought to light as children emulate our behaviors and copy our patterns of speech.

Children need parents to teach, train, nurture, and disciple them. Parents need children to become more like Christ. This process of being changed into His image is called sanctification. Being responsible for the care of kids around the clock, twenty-four hours a day, three hundred sixty-five days a year for generations, not only provides a lot of feedback for our character development, it changes us as we give ourselves to our families.

One of my favorite passages describing being poured out for others is found in an obscure passage in Jeremiah. "Moab has been at ease from his youth and has settled on his dregs; he has not been emptied from vessel to vessel, nor has he gone into exile; so his taste remains in him, and his scent is not changed." (Jeremiah 48:11) Being poured out for others, transforms us. We are not the same person after being emptied and pouring out our life for our children.

There is a man who lived three hundred sixty-five years. His name is Enoch. We read about him in Genesis and Hebrews. "By faith Enoch was taken up so that he should not see death, and he was not found, because God had taken him. Now before he was taken he was commended as having pleased God." (Hebrews 11:5)

"When Enoch had lived 65 years, he fathered Methuselah. Enoch walked with God after he fathered Methuselah 300 years and had other sons and daughters. Thus all the days of Enoch were 365 years. Enoch walked with God, and he was not, for God took him." (Genesis 5:21–24)

Enoch did not die, but was translated. Enoch walked with God "after" he fathered Methuselah. We are not told what went on in Enoch's heart when he became a father to Methuselah, but perhaps having a son was just the impetus he needed to walk with God in a deeper way. Maybe having a son and seeking to train him to love God and His word caused him to search his own heart.

Several years ago, I was reading Deuteronomy 6:7 about teaching my children diligently. My attention was directed to the two preceding verses informing me that until I love God and His word with everything in me, I will not be equipped to teach my children to love God or the word. This insight motivated me to begin a journey of seeking God earnestly which led to the hardest and best year of my life. This life changing journey was due in part, to my desire to be a better dad.

Family is a God idea. He designed this sacred institution to help us pass our faith on to our children, and to become more like Jesus in the process. The divine transformation of our character is an essential byproduct of the DNA of family. "For this is the will of God, your sanctification." (1 Thessalonians 4:3) As we assimilate how much God in Christ loves us, and with eyes on Jesus, see to love each other as we have been loved, we become more like Him.

Transformation does not occur by looking in a mirror. Real change occurs by fixing our attention on Christ. A wise man once said, "One look at self and I am horrified, one look at Him I am glorified."

God's will is for each of His children to be changed, from our hearts, as we love God and others. We were created in His image, but we fell. As we believe the good news and are born from above with the help of His Spirit, we become new creatures. "Those whom he foreknew He also predestined to be conformed to the image of His Son." (Romans 8:29) We were chosen and called to be changed.

This lifelong process begins at our rebirth and continues throughout the the valleys and mountaintops of life. "We all, with unveiled face, beholding the glory of the Lord, are being transformed into the same image from one degree of glory to another. For this comes from the Lord who is the Spirit." (2 Corinthians 3:18)

Be encouraged. If you have read "The Great Stone Face," remember the boy who became a godly man. By fixing his attention fully upon the character and visage of the wise and Godly man who was to come, became the fulfillment of the prophecy. Often the progress is not readily evident to us, but obvious to others. As we pursue Christ, we are being changed from glory to glory.

"The Great Stone Face" is a beautiful illustration, but it falls short in that the stone is lifeless, while our God lives. Our Dad exudes life, joy, peace, acceptance, love. His radiant countenance is turned towards us and welcome us while His eyes convey love, compassion, joy, and acceptance.

This process of being incrementally transformed is similar to the motion of the head of a ratchet. As the handle swings vigorously back and forth, the wrench steadily moves in the same direction to tighten or loosen the nut. Do not lose heart. Life moves us in many directions, but God is steadfastly conforming us to the image of His Son.

While we are adopted children of God, by faith in Jesus, we embrace the hope we shall one day be wonderfully altered when we see Him face to face. "Beloved, we are God's children now, and what we will be has not yet appeared; but we know that when he appears we shall be like him, because we shall see him as he is. And everyone who thus hopes in him purifies himself as he is pure." (1 John 3:2–3)

"When I was young I set out to change the world. When I grew a little older, I perceived this was too ambitious, so I set out to change my state. This too I realized was too ambitious, so I set out to change my own town. When I realized I could not even do this, I tried to change my family. Now as an old man I know I should have started by changing myself. If I had started by changing myself, maybe then I would have succeeded in changing my family, the town, and even the state, and who knows maybe even the world." These words, attributed to Hasidic Rabbi Israel Salanter on his deathbed, are found in The Daily Office, week 3 day 5, by Peter Scazzero.

As much as we might desire to be changed, we cannot change ourselves. "I know, O Lord, that the way of man is not in himself, that it is not in man who walks to direct his steps." (Jeremiah 10:23) The expression in John 3:3 frequently translated "born again" can also be rendered "born from above" which I believe is more accurate. Born from above is more consistent with the thought expressed in James 1:17. "Every good gift and every perfect gift is from above, coming down from the Father of lights with whom there is no variation or shadow due to change."

By the Spirit we are convicted of sin (John 16:8) and only by the Spirit are we able to declare Jesus is Lord (1 Corinthians 12:3). The same Spirit effects significant change in our heart. We may modify our behavior and alter the way we act, but these temporary changes will not produce long term transformation.

New birth includes death. "Truly, truly, I say to you, unless a grain of wheat falls into the earth and dies, it remains alone; but if it dies, it bears much fruit." (John 12:24) Within the family dynamic there are ample opportunities to lay one's own preferences aside and deny oneself. These daily opportunities to deny ourself and take up our cross are making us more like our savior. The little choices we make and these light momentary afflictions are "preparing for us an eternal weight of glory beyond all comparison." (2 Corinthians 4:17)

I was an earnest, committed believer with wonderful training in college and seminary under Godly men and women. I mistakenly assumed my passion and education would be sufficient to bring about the goal I had on my heart, raising children who would love God and extend His kingdom. I assumed God gave these four sons to Sandi and me so we could train and teach them. Looking back now, I recognize I had no idea of the levels of change God wanted to effect in my own life, and to what degree He would use my children and my wife to

teach me. I was not just an agent of change, I was in
need of change! Now I recognize it is God's design
for a family to learn from each other, and refine one
another's character making us more like our master.

It was thirty-three years later when I grasped in
a deeper way, the concept of grace. I now am rooted
and grounded in God in a way I never dreamed
possible. I had lived a life of striving, trying, and
never feeling like I measured up, while regularly
battling condemnation. I now know God likes me. I
learned this from my family.

I also know I have a lot of pain and scars from
my childhood. This baggage is not going away with
age or new accomplishments. It has to be faced and
embraced with truth and the help of other people. I
learned this with the help and patience of my wife
and children. Hurt people, hurt other people. I was
a hurt man. I am being changed by the help of the
Spirit, by the word of God. If it is true that hurt
people, hurt people, then perhaps it is also true that
loved people, love people. For the more I am loved
and liked by my Dad, the more I love and like others.

The more I seek to grow deeper into the love
of God and be rooted and grounded in His grace
and affection, the more ability I have to reflect and
ask God to search my heart. David prayed, "Search
me, O God, and know my heart! Try me and know
my thoughts! And see if there be any grievous
way in me, and lead me in the way everlasting!"
(Psalms 139:23–24) "Grievous way" may also be
translated "way of pain."

. Even if I had known this truth years ago, I doubt if I would have given God permission to search my heart and reveal the sources of my pain. However as He has revealed His care and affection for me, I am more willing to let Him work deeper in my inner man. The more I let God work in my heart the more I am transformed into his image.

With God's help and encouragement, I am seeking know the love of Christ in a new way while growing in the grace and knowledge of Jesus. I am pursuing God through His Word and seeking His person to taste and experience His goodness. I have this deep desire to let my roots grow deeper in the love and affection of God, for when I have deeper roots I will experience better fruit. I believe that the more I find my needs met in Jesus, the better equipped I will be to love God, love my family, and love others as I have been loved. (based on Ephesians 3:14–20, 2 Peter 3:18, Psalm 34:8)

Prayer

"May the God of peace himself sanctify you completely, and may your whole spirit and soul and body be kept blameless at the coming of our Lord Jesus Christ. He who calls you is faithful; he will surely do it." (1 Thessalonians 5:23–24)

QUESTIONS FOR REFLECTION AND STUDY

1. How have your children provided you with accountability?

2. As Steve sought raise children who love God and extend his kingdom, what did he find out was God's design for family?

3. What do we need to do before we can teach our children to love God & His Word?

4. Do you think there is truth in the statement, "hurt people, hurt people", and conversely, "loved people, can truly love people"? Can you give specific examples where you have seen this lived out?

5. What is the relationship between knowing God's love in a real, experiential way and asking him to search our hearts, reveal our pain, and transform us to be more like him?

CHAPTER 13: BY THIS SHALL ALL MEN KNOW

When God worked in my heart and I recommitted my life to follow Him fully in college, my life verse became Matthew 6:33, "Seek first the kingdom of God and his righteousness, and all these things will be added to you." Upon graduation from Grove City College, I attended Gordon-Conwell Theological Seminary as preparation for seeking first the Kingdom.

While there I took several classes on the world mission of the church and personal evangelism from Dr. J. Christy Wilson, Jr. I learned about the needs of the world and made supplication for them during our lunch time prayer gatherings. It was then I heard the Great Commission, which is mentioned in each of the four gospels and the Book of Acts.

"Jesus came and said to them, 'All authority in heaven and on earth has been given to me. Go therefore and make disciples of all nations, baptizing them in the name of the Father and of the Son and of the Holy Spirit, teaching them to observe all that I have commanded you. And behold, I am with you always, to the end of the age.'" (Matthew 28:18-20)

"Repentance and forgiveness of sins should be proclaimed in his name to all nations, beginning from Jerusalem. You are witnesses of these things. And behold, I am sending the promise of my Father upon you. But stay in the city until you are clothed with power from on high." (Luke 24:47–49)

"He said to them, 'Go into all the world and proclaim the gospel to the whole creation.'" (Mark 16:15)

"Jesus said to them again, 'Peace be with you. As the Father has sent me, even so I am sending you.'" (John 20:21)

"You will receive power when the Holy Spirit has come upon you, and you will be my witnesses in Jerusalem and in all Judea and Samaria, and to the end of the earth." (Acts 1:8)

While I have been willing to go wherever God moved me, I have not been led to serve as a missionary in a different part of the world. But my heart is still on the field which is ripe for harvest and I am believing for the day when "Every knee will bow and every tongue confess that Jesus Christ is Lord, to the glory of God the Father." (Philippians 2:10–11)

The day after I graduated from seminary I was married to Sandra. Within a year, Isaac was born, followed by Ethan, Joseph, and John. During those early years I wore many hats, serving as an assistant to the pastor of a small church, as a youth leader, as a summer camp director for teens, and as a Junior and Senior High School math teacher. My ministry field was primarily young people. I came to the conclusion that while we all need encouragement in our walk with God, the most important influence in the life of young people was their parents. Programs were helpful and camps were special, but you can't replace mom and dad. My eyes were opening to the role of the family in the greater plan of God.

While I was in seminary I had taken a few classes on Christian Education. This was in the late 1970s, after prayer had been taken out of the public schools and there was a growing movement of Christian Schools as a reaction to God being asked to leave government education. For my term paper I wrote about what scripture had to say about education. I did not read books or consult what others thought about this topic, I just read scripture.

I was using a large *Young's Concordance* since we did not have personal computers (if you are under thirty ask an older person to see what this might look like). I looked up every word I could think of pertaining to learning and education, "teach," "teacher," "teaching," "instructor," "instruction," etc. After doing my research I came to the conclusion from scripture, parents were to be the primary instructors of their children and the curriculum should be based on the inspired word of God.

Through work with youth and study of the scripture I began to see more about the importance of the family which God designed. I also make it a practice to read through the Bible from Genesis to Revelation each year. As I read Genesis each January, I recognize after God created the world in six days, His next sovereign act was to take one man and one woman, the first couple, Adam and Eve, and make them one flesh. He then commissioned them to be fruitful and multiply and fill the earth.

This sacred institution called the family, which

consists of one man and one woman, is not simply a good idea, it is a God idea. He created it. Before Abraham, Moses, the nation of Israel, or the church, two people, one male and one female, were made one.

As a father and husband I have diligently studied scripture to see the plan for the family. In the New Testament, Ephesians 5 is the *Magna Carta* for the home. In the Old Testament, the book of Deuteronomy has the most significant passages directing my efforts as a father. I call Deuteronomy 6:4–7 the divine blueprint for the home. "Hear, O Israel: The Lord our God, the Lord is one. You shall love the Lord your God with all your heart and with all your soul and with all your might. And these words that I command you today shall be on your heart. You shall teach them diligently to your children, and shall talk of them when you sit in your house, and when you walk by the way, and when you lie down, and when you rise."

For many years I would think and consider how God would have me apply the seventh verse. What did it mean to teach my children diligently? How did I talk of the commandments while I sit, walk, lie down, and rise in our home? Eventually we began meeting for regular times of family worship. I wrote about this in *Family Worship*.

Then Sandi and I felt moved to home educate our sons. I surmised this was one way I could talk of the commandments while I sit, walk, lie down, and rise.

Many years later I was asked why I spoke so

much about the seventh verse but did not mention verses five and six. As I read these passages I saw that before I could teach my children to love God and His Word, I needed to love God with everything in me and love His word myself. This revelation led me to begin asking God to help me love Him with all my heart, soul, mind, and strength.

I was expecting a rekindling or reviving in my own heart for God. Instead He began to communicate through various sources, how much He loved me. This is consistent with 1 John 4:19. "We love because He first loved us." The inspired verse which made the most difference in this journey to know and assimilate the love of God was, and is, John 15:9. "As the Father has loved me, so have I loved you. Abide in my love."

Then a few verses later Jesus says "As I have loved you, love one another." This is called the new commandment. "A new commandment I give to you, that you love one another: just as I have loved you, you also are to love one another. By this all people will know that you are my disciples, if you have love for one another." John 13:34-35

These verses in John have led me to create a phrase to define a new concept, the Great HomeMission. By modifying the Great Commission, I am suggesting before we go into all the world, we practice the new commandment with our family. As we learn to love one another as we have been loved, within the home, we will profoundly and effectively impact the church and the world. All people will know we are His disciples as we love one another, as God has loved us.

The rest of this chapter will be addressing the incredible potential God implanted and invested in the family unit.

As a Christian, my first responsibility is to love God. As a husband, I am commanded to love my wife as Christ loved the church (Ephesians 5:25). I am unable to fulfill either of these tasks unless and until I am first loved by God (1 John 4:19). I also see this same order at work in the way Jesus prepared to fulfill His ministry and purpose. God the Father loved Jesus the Son. He affirmed His divine affection for His beloved Son, affirmed His identity at His baptism, and gave Him the Holy Spirit (Matthew 3:16-17).

It was the love of the Father for the world, which motivated Him to send Jesus to the earth to die for us. "For God so loved the world, that He gave His only begotten Son ..." (John 3:16) It was the love of the Father poured into Jesus which enabled Him to love us the same way. "As the Father has loved me, so have I loved you. Abide in my love." (John 15:9)

Near the conclusion of His earthly ministry, Jesus took His disciples aside and told them to wait in Jerusalem, until they too would be baptized with the Holy Spirit. After which they were to be His witnesses from Jerusalem to the ends of the earth. "While staying with them He ordered them not to depart from Jerusalem, but to wait for the promise of the Father, which, He said, 'you heard from me; for John baptized with water, but you will be baptized

with the Holy Spirit not many days from now.'"
(Acts 1:4-5)

Jerusalem First

"You will receive power when the Holy Spirit has
come upon you, and you will be my witnesses in
Jerusalem and in all Judea and Samaria, and to the
end of the earth." (Acts 1:8)

Geographically, Jerusalem is the center of
concentric circles. As you move away from the
center, you encounter Judea next, then Samaria,
and finally the end of the earth. This is the way the
disciples conducted their ministry. They were faithful
at home and eventually reached the world.

We are also called to think globally, but begin
locally. We carry the great commission in our heart,
but begin by faithfully fulfilling our obligations in
Jerusalem. Jerusalem to me is my family. One of the
reasons I have this conviction is because of these
passages in 1 Timothy 3 and 5.

"He (the bishop or overseer) must manage his
own household well, with all dignity keeping his
children submissive, for if someone does not know
how to manage his own household, how will he care
for God's church?" (1 Timothy 3:4-5)

Paul is instructing Timothy how to set up the
leadership structure in the local church. After
enumerating several other prerequisites, he ends by
saying if the man is not able to be a servant leader
in his own home he will not know how to serve in
the church. He never mentions their education, their

gifts, or their abilities. He focuses instead on what kind of a husband and father the candidate is.

Before men are to assume a position in the local church they must have learned to practice their faith with those who are closest to them. I think of what Jesus said, "Well done, good and faithful servant. You have been faithful over a little; I will set you over much." (Matthew 25:23) We are not prepared and equipped for ministry by what we learn in a classroom, but by how we interact, love, and forgive our wife and children.

Similar instructions are mentioned for deacons.

"Let deacons each be the husband of one wife, managing their children and their own households well. For those who serve well as deacons gain a good standing for themselves and also great confidence in the faith that is in Christ Jesus." (1 Timothy 3:12–13)

Two chapters later, Paul exhorts Timothy to treat the members of the church as they have done within the context of a healthy family. "Do not rebuke an older man but encourage him as you would a father, younger men as brothers, older women as mothers, younger women as sisters, in all purity." (1 Timothy 5:1–2)

It is self evident that men who are inspired to diligently serve at home, will lead better at church. It is equally true that healthy God-fearing families are the foundation for vital flourishing churches. As men are rooted and grounded in the love of God and learn to love as they have been loved, their wife and children will be strengthened and encouraged. When we begin in Jerusalem, the family and the local church will be built up by a father and husband who loves God and God's word.

The call to be a witness to the world is in John.

"As the Father has sent me, even so I am sending you." (John 20:21) The Father sent Jesus, rooted and grounded in love, assured of His identity as God's Son, and filled with the Spirit. In the same way, we are to be sent, just **AS** Jesus was sent. As we "comprehend with all the saints what is the breadth and length and height and depth, and to know the love of Christ that surpasses knowledge," we too will "be filled with all the fullness of God." (Ephesians 3:18–19)

As believers grow in their capacity to walk in the fullness of His love, and love one another as Jesus has loved us, our witness will be known by the world. "By this all people will know that you are my disciples, if you have love for one another." (John 13:35)

The Great Commission commences with the Great HomeMission. May God make us faithful to His plan and purpose.

Prayer

"The grace of the Lord Jesus Christ and the love of God and the fellowship of the Holy Spirit be with you all." (2 Corinthians 13:14)

QUESTIONS FOR REFLECTION AND STUDY

1. Describe the Great HomeMission. Do you think it would work? Why or why not?
2. What is the divine order in Deuteronomy 6:5–7?
3. Describe how Jerusalem in the Great Commission can be likened to our family.
4. What scriptures does Steve use to demonstrate how important it is for believers to experience God's love and transformation in the context of a family?
5. How will all people know that we are disciples?

APPENDIX A:
HOW HAS JESUS LOVED US?

Jesus was pierced and crushed for our sin.

"He was pierced for our transgressions; He was crushed for our iniquities." (Isaiah 53:5)

Jesus heals us.

"With His wounds we are healed." (Isaiah 53:5)

Jesus is with us.

"The virgin shall conceive and bear a son, and they shall call his name Immanuel (which means, God with us)." (Mathew 1:23)

Jesus bears our burdens.

"Come to me, all who labor and are heavy laden, and I will give you rest." (Matthew 11:28)

*Jesus is gentle and lowly. His yoke
is easy, His burden is light.*

"Take my yoke upon you, and learn from me, for I am gentle and lowly in heart, and you will find rest for your souls. For my yoke is easy, and my burden is light." (Matthew 11:29-30)

Jesus encourages us.

"Look at My Servant, whom I have chosen. He is My Beloved, who pleases Me. I will put My Spirit upon Him, and He will proclaim justice to the nations. He will not fight or shout or raise His voice in public. He will not crush the weakest reed or put out a flickering can-dle." (Matthew 12:18-20, NLT)

Jesus is present.

"Where two or three are gathered in My name, there am I among them." (Matthew 18:20)

Jesus came to serve.

"Jesus called them to him and said, 'You know that the rulers of the Gentiles lord it over them, and their great ones exercise authority over them. It shall not be so among you. But whoever would be great among you must be your servant, and whoever would be first among you must be your slave, even as the Son of Man came not to be served but to serve, and to give his life as a ransom for many.'" (Matthew 20:25–28)

Jesus is with us always.

"I am with you always, to the end of the age." (Matthew 28:20)

"Even though I walk through the valley of the shadow of death, I will fear no evil, for You are with me; Your rod and Your staff, they comfort me." (Psalm 23:4)

Jesus gives us a hundredfold life now.

"Jesus said, 'Truly, I say to you, there is no one who has left house or brothers or sisters or mother or father or children or lands, for my sake and for the gospel, who will not re-ceive a hundredfold now in this time." (Mark 10:29–30)

Jesus reveals the Father to us.

"No one knows who the Son is except the Father, or who the Father is except the Son and anyone to whom the Son chooses to reveal Him." (Luke 10:22)

"Whoever has seen Me has seen the Father."
(John 14:9)

"He is the image of the invisible God, the firstborn of all creation." (Colossians 1:15)

Jesus seeks us.

"The Son of Man came to seek and to save the lost." (Luke 19:10)

Jesus forgives us.

"Jesus said, 'Father, forgive them, for they know not what they do.'" (Luke 23:34)

Jesus takes away our sin.

"Behold, the Lamb of God, who takes away the sin of the world" (John 1:29)

Jesus understands us.

"Jesus on His part did not entrust himself to them, because He knew all people and needed no one to bear witness about man, for He Himself knew what was in man." (John 2:24–25)

Jesus gives believers eternal life.

"Anyone who believes in God's Son has eternal life." (John 3:36)

Jesus satisfies our thirst.

"Whoever drinks of the water that I will give him will never be thirsty again. The water that I will give him will become in him a spring of water welling up to eternal life." (John 4:14)

Jesus is the bread of life.

"I am the bread of life. Your fathers ate the manna in the wilderness, and they died. This is the bread that comes down from heaven, so that one may eat of it and not die. I am the living bread that came down from heaven. If anyone eats of this bread, he will live for-ever." (John 6:48–51)

Jesus provides believers living water.

"Whoever believes in Me, as the Scripture has said, 'Out of his heart will flow rivers of living water.'" (John 7:38)

Jesus gives us abundant life.

"I came that they may have life and have it abundantly." (John 10:10)

*Jesus gives everlasting life and keeps
His disciples in His hand.*

"I give them eternal life, and they will never perish, and no one will snatch them out of my hand." (John 10:28)

Jesus loves us to the end.

"When Jesus knew that His hour had come to depart out of this world to the Father, having loved His own who were in the world, He loved them to the end." (John 13:1)

*Jesus prepares a place for His bride
and is coming back for her.*

"If I go and prepare a place for you, I will come again and will take you to myself, that where I am you may be also." (John 14:3)

Jesus sends the Spirit to be with us forever.

"I will ask the Father, and he will give you another Helper, to be with you forever." (John 14:16)

Jesus makes us clean through the word.

"Already you are clean because of the word that I have spoken to you." (John 15:3)

"He might sanctify her, having cleansed her by the washing of water with the word." (Ephesians 5:26)

Jesus loves us perfectly.

"As the Father has loved Me, so have I loved you. Abide in My love." (John 15:9)

Jesus gives us the Word of God.

"I have given them Your Word." (John 17:14)

Jesus reveals the Father's name
and His love to His children.

"I made known to them Your name, and I will continue to make it known, that the love with which You have loved Me may be in them, and I in them." (John 17:26)

Jesus has purchased me with His blood.

"Take heed therefore unto yourselves, and to all the flock, over the which the Holy Ghost hath made you overseers, to feed the church of God, which he hath purchased with his own blood." (Acts 20:28 KJV)

"You were bought with a price. So glorify God in your body." (1 Corinthians 6:20)

Jesus died for us when we were weak and sinful.

"While we were still weak, at the right time Christ died for the ungodly. For one will scarcely die for a righteous person—though perhaps for a good person one would dare even to die— but God shows His love for us in that while we were still sinners, Christ died for us." (Romans 5:6–8)

Jesus justified us by His blood and saves us from the wrath of God.

"Since, therefore, we have now been justified by His blood, much more shall we be saved by Him from the wrath of God." (Romans 5:9)

Jesus reconciles us to God while we were enemies.

"While we were enemies we were reconciled to God by the death of His Son." (Romans 5:10a)

Jesus saves us by His life.

"Much more, now that we are reconciled, shall we be saved by His life." (Romans 5:10b)

Jesus gives us the gift of righteousness to reign with Him.

"Much more those who receive the abundance of grace and of the gift of righteousness will reign in life through the One, Jesus Christ." (Romans 5:17)

Jesus baptizes us into His death so
we may walk in newness of life.

"Do you not know that all of us who have been baptized into Christ Jesus were baptized into His death? We were buried therefore with Him by baptism into death, in order that, just as Christ was raised from the dead by the glory of the Father, we too might walk in newness of life." (Romans 6:3–4)

Jesus united us with Him in His
death and resurrection.

"If we have been united with Him in a death like His, we shall certainly be united with Him in a resurrection likeHis." (Romans 6:5)

Jesus crucifies our old self to free us from sin.

"We know that our old self was crucified with Him in order that the body of sin might be brought to nothing, so that we would no longer be enslaved to sin." (Romans 6:6)

Jesus gives us eternal life.

"The wages of sin is death, but the free gift of God is eternal life in Christ Jesus our Lord." (Romans 6:23)

Jesus delivers us from condemnation.

"There is therefore now no condemnation for those who are in Christ Jesus ." (Romans 8:1)

Jesus gives us the mind of Christ.

"But we have the mind of Christ." (1 Corinthians 2:16)

Jesus always leads in victory and uses
us to spread His divine fragrance.

"Thanks be to God, who in Christ always leads us in triumphal procession, and through us spreads the fragrance of the knowledge of Him everywhere." (2 Corinthians 2:14)

Jesus makes us new creatures.

"Wherefore if any man is in Christ, he is a new creature: the old things are passed away; behold, they are become new." (2 Corinthians 5:17)

Jesus was made sin for us.

"For our sake he made Him to be sin who knew no sin." (2 Corinthians 5:21a)

Jesus makes us the righteousness of God.

"So that in Him we might become the righteousness of God." (2 Corinthians 5:21b)

Jesus became poor that we might be rich.

"You know the grace of our Lord Jesus Christ, that though He was rich, yet for your sake He became poor, so that you by His poverty might become rich." (2 Corinthians 8:9)

Jesus lives in us.

"I have been crucified with Christ. It is no longer I who live, but Christ who lives in me." (Galatians 2:20)

Jesus gave Himself up for us.

"Walk in love, even as Christ also loved you, and gave Himself up for us." (Ephesians 5:2)

Jesus laid His life down for us.

"Husbands, love your wives, as Christ loved the church and gave himself up for her." (Ephesians 5:25)

Jesus created us.

"By Him all things were created, ... all things were created through Him and for Him." (Colossians 1:16)

Jesus holds all things together.

"He is before all things, and in Him all things hold together." (Colossians 1:17)

Jesus became human, humbled Himself, and died for us.

"Being found in human form, He humbled Himself by becoming obedient to the point of death, even death on a cross." (Philippians 2:8)

Jesus abolished death and brought eternal life.

"Our Savior Christ Jesus , who abolished death and brought life and immortality to light through the gospel." (2 Timothy 1:10)

Jesus saves us according to His mercy.

"When the goodness and loving kindness of God our Savior appeared, He saved us, not because of works done by us in righteousness, but according to His own mercy." (Titus 3:4–5)

Jesus is a compassionate and accessible priest.

"Since then we have a great high priest who has passed through the heavens, Jesus , the Son of God, let us hold fast our confession. For we do not have a high priest who is unable to sympathize with our weaknesses, but One who in every respect has been tempted as we are, yet without sin. Let us then with confidence draw near to the throne of grace, that we may receive mercy and find grace to help in time of need." (Hebrews 4:14–16)

Jesus prays for us.

"He always lives to make intercession for them." (Hebrews 7:25)

"Christ Jesus is the one who died—more than that, who was raised who is at the right hand of God, who indeed is interceding for us." (Romans 8:34)

Jesus purifies us from sin.

"How much more will the blood of Christ, who through the eternal Spirit offered Him-self without blemish to God, purify our conscience from dead works to serve the living God." (Hebrews 9:14)

Jesus never abandons us.

"God has said, 'I will never fail you. I will never abandon you.'" (Hebrews 13:5 NLT)

Jesus is our helper.

"We can say with confidence, 'The LORD is my helper, so I will have no fear.'" (Hebrews 13:6 NLT)

"The LORD is my shepherd; I have all that I need." (Psalm 23:1 NLT)

Jesus never changes.

"Jesus Christ is the same yesterday and today and forever." (Hebrews 13:8)

Jesus is good and kind.

"When the goodness and loving kindness of God our Savior appeared." (Titus 3:4)

Jesus forgives and cleanses us from sin.

"If we confess our sins, He is faithful and just to forgive us our sins and to cleanse us from all unrighteousness." (1 John 1:9)

Jesus is our eternal advocate.

"If anyone does sin, we have an advocate with the Father, Jesus Christ the righteous." (1 John 2:1)

Jesus destroyed the works of the devil.

"Son of God appeared ... that He might destroy the works of the devil." (1 John 3:8)

Jesus laid his life down for us.

"By this we know love, that He laid down his life for us." (1 John 3:16)

Jesus gives us grace, mercy, and peace.

"Grace, mercy, and peace will be with us, from God the Father and from Jesus Christ the Father's Son, in truth and love." (2 John 3)

Jesus has freed us from our sins by His blood.

"To him who loves us and has freed us from our sins by His blood." (Revelation 1:5)

Jesus made us a kingdom and
priests to our Father God.

"And made us a kingdom, priests to His God and Father, to Him be glory and dominion forever and ever. Amen." (Revelation 1:6)

Jesus has called and chosen us.

"They will make war on the Lamb, and the Lamb will conquer them, for He is Lord of lords and King of kings, and those with Him are called and chosen and faithful." (Revelation 17:14)

Jesus is committed to marrying us.

"Let us rejoice and exult and give him the glory, for the marriage of the Lamb has come, and his Bride has made herself ready." (Revelation 19:7)

APPENDIX B: "THE GREAT STONE FACE"

From *The Snow-Image, and Other Twice-Told Tales*, 1851, 1852

By Nathaniel Hawthorne, 1804–1864

ONE AFTERNOON, when the sun was going down, a mother and her little boy sat at the door of their cottage, talking about the Great Stone Face. They had but to lift their eyes, and there it was plainly to be seen, though miles away, with the sunshine brightening all its features.

And what was the Great Stone Face?

Embosomed amongst a family of lofty mountains, there was a valley so spacious that it contained many thousand inhabitants. Some of these good people dwelt in log huts, with the black forest all around them, on the steep and difficult hill-sides. Others had their homes in comfortable farm-houses, and cultivated the rich soil on the gentle slopes or level surfaces of the valley. Others, again, were congregated into populous villages, where some wild, highland rivulet, tumbling down from its birthplace in the upper mountain region, had been caught and tamed by human cunning, and compelled to turn the machinery of cotton factories. The inhabitants of this valley, in short, were numerous, and of many modes of life. But all of them, grown people and children, had a kind of familiarity with the Great Stone Face, although some possessed the gift of distinguishing this grand natural phenomenon more perfectly than many of their neighbors.

The Great Stone Face, then, was a work of Nature in her mood of majestic playfulness, formed on the perpendicular side of a mountain by some immense rocks, which had been thrown together in such a position as, when viewed at a proper distance, precisely to resemble the features of the human countenance. It seemed as if an enormous giant, or a Titan, had sculptured his own likeness on the precipice. There was the broad arch of the forehead, a hundred feet in height; the nose, with its long bridge; and the vast lips, which, if they could have spoken, would have rolled their thunder accents from one end of the valley to the other. True it is, that if the spectator approached too near, he lost the outline of the gigantic visage, and could discern only a heap of ponderous and gigantic rocks, piled in chaotic ruin one upon another. Retracing his steps, however, the wondrous features would again be seen; and the further he withdrew from them, the more like a human face, with all its original divinity intact, did they appear; until, as it grew dim in the distance, with the clouds and glorified vapor of the mountains clustering about it, the Great Stone Face seemed positively to be alive.

It was a happy lot for children to grow up to manhood or womanhood with the Great Stone Face before their eyes, for all the features were noble, and the expression was at once grand and sweet, as if it were the glow of a vast, warm heart, that embraced all mankind in its affections, and had room for more. It was an education only to look at it. According to the belief of many people, the valley owed much of its fertility to this benign aspect that was continually beaming over it, illuminating the clouds, and infusing its tenderness into the sunshine.

As we began with saying, a mother and her little boy sat at their cottage door, gazing at the Great Stone Face, and talking about it. The child's name

was Ernest.

"Mother, said he, while the Titanic visage smiled on him, "I wish that it could speak, for it looks so very kindly that its voice must needs be pleasant. If I were to see a man with such a face, I should love him dearly."

"If an old prophecy should come to pass," answered his mother, "we may see a man, some time or other, with exactly such a face as that."

"What prophecy do you mean, dear mother?" eagerly inquired Ernest. "Pray tell me all about it!"

So his mother told him a story that her own mother had told to her, when she herself was younger than little Ernest; a story, not of things that were past, but of what was yet to come; a story, nevertheless, so very old, that even the Indians, who formerly inhabited this valley, had heard it from their forefathers, to whom, as they affirmed, it had been murmured by the mountain streams, and whispered by the wind among the tree-tops. The purport was, that, at some future day, a child should be born hereabouts, who was destined to become the greatest and noblest personage of his time, and whose countenance, in manhood, should bear an exact resemblance to the Great Stone Face. Not a few old-fashioned people, and young ones likewise, in the ardor of their hopes, still cherished an enduring faith in this old prophecy. But others, who had seen more of the world, had watched and waited till they were weary, and had beheld no man with such a face, nor any man that proved to be much greater or nobler than his neighbors, concluded it to be nothing but an idle tale. At all events, the great man of the prophecy had not yet appeared.

"O, mother, dear mother!" cried Ernest, clapping his hands above his head, I do hope that I shall live to see him!"

His mother was an affectionate and thoughtful woman, and felt that it was wisest not to discourage the generous hopes of her little boy. So she only said to him, "Perhaps you may."

And Ernest never forgot the story that his mother told him. It was always in his mind, whenever he looked upon the Great Stone Face. He spent his childhood in the log-cottage where he was born, and was dutiful to his mother, and helpful to her in many things, assisting her much with his little hands, and more with his loving heart. In this manner, from a happy yet often pensive child, he grew up to be a mild, quiet, unobtrusive boy, and sun-browned with labor in the fields, but with more intelligence brightening his aspect than is seen in many lads who have been taught at famous schools. Yet Ernest had had no teacher, save only that the Great Stone Face became one to him. When the toil of the day was over, he would gaze at it for hours, until he began to imagine that those vast features recognized him, and gave him a smile of kindness and encouragement, responsive to his own look of veneration. We must not take upon us to affirm that this was a mistake, although the Face may have looked no more kindly at Ernest than at all the world besides. But the secret was, that the boy's tender and confiding simplicity discerned what other people could not see; and thus the love, which was meant for all, became his peculiar portion.

About this time, there went a rumor throughout the valley, that the great man, foretold from ages long ago, who was to bear a resemblance to the Great Stone Face, had appeared at last. It seems that, many years before, a young man had migrated from the valley and settled at a distant seaport, where, after getting together a little money, he had set up as a shopkeeper. His name—but I could never learn whether it was his real one, or a

nickname that had grown out of his habits and success
in life—was Gathergold. Being shrewd and active, and
endowed by Providence with that inscrutable faculty which
develops itself in what the world calls luck, he became
an exceedingly rich merchant, and owner of a whole fleet
of bulky-bottomed ships. All the countries of the globe
appeared to join hands for the mere purpose of adding
heap after heap to the mountainous accumulation of this
one man's wealth. The cold regions of the north, almost
within the gloom and shadow of the Arctic Circle, sent him
their tribute in the shape of furs; hot Africa sifted for him
the golden sands of her rivers, and gathered up the ivory
tusks of her great elephants out of the forests; the East
came bringing him the rich shawls, and spices, and teas,
and the effulgence of diamonds, and the gleaming purity
of large pearls. The ocean, not to be behindhand with the
earth, yielded up her mighty whales, that Mr. Gathergold
might sell their oil, and make a profit on it. Be the original
commodity what it might, it was gold within his grasp.
It might be said of him, as of Midas in the fable, that
whatever he touched with his finger immediately glistened,
and grew yellow, and was changed at once into sterling
metal, or, which suited him still better, into piles of coin.
And, when Mr. Gathergold had become so very rich that
it would have taken him a hundred years only to count
his wealth, he bethought himself of his native valley, and
resolved to go back thither, and end his days where he was
born. With this purpose in view, he sent a skillful architect
to build him such a palace as should be fit for a man of his
vast wealth to live in.

As I have said above, it had already been rumored in
the valley that Mr. Gathergold had turned out to be the
prophetic personage so long and vainly looked for, and
that his visage was the perfect and undeniable similitude
of the Great Stone Face. People were the more ready to
believe that this must needs be the fact, when they beheld
the splendid edifice that rose, as if by enchantment, on
the site of his father's old weather-beaten farm-house. The
exterior was of marble, so dazzlingly white that it seemed
as though the whole structure might melt away in the
sunshine, like those humbler ones which Mr. Gathergold,
in his young play-days, before his fingers were gifted with
the touch of transmutation, had been accustomed to build
of snow. It had a richly ornamented portico, supported
by tall pillars, beneath which was a lofty door, studded
with silver knobs, and made of a kind of variegated wood

that had been brought from beyond the sea. The windows, from the floor to the ceiling of each stately apartment, were composed, respectively, of but one enormous pane of glass, so transparently pure that it was said to be a finer medium than even the vacant atmosphere. Hardly anybody had been permitted to see the interior of this palace; but it was reported, and with good semblance of truth, to be far more gorgeous than the outside, insomuch that whatever was iron or brass in other houses, was silver or gold in this; and Mr. Gathergold's bed-chamber, especially, made such a glittering appearance that no ordinary man would have been able to close his eyes there. But, on the other hand, Mr. Gathergold was now so inured to wealth, that perhaps he could not have closed his eyes unless where the gleam of it was certain to find its way beneath his eyelids.

In due time, the mansion was finished; next came the upholsterers, with magnificent furniture; then, a whole troop of black and white servants, the harbingers of Mr. Gathergold, who, in his own majestic person was expected to arrive at sunset. Our friend Ernest, meanwhile, had been deeply stirred by the idea that the great man, the noble man, the man of prophecy, after so many ages of delay, was at length to be made manifest to his native valley. He knew, boy as he was, that there were a thousand ways in which Mr. Gathergold, with his vast wealth, might transform himself into an angel of beneficence, and assume a control over human affairs as wide and benignant as the smile of the Great Stone Face. Full of faith and hope, Ernest doubted not that what the people said was true, and that now he was to behold the living likeness of those wondrous features on the mountain-side. While the boy was still gazing up the valley, and fancying, as he always did, that the Great Stone Face returned his gaze and looked kindly at him, the rumbling of wheels was heard, approaching swiftly along the winding road.

"Here he comes!" cried a group of people who were assembled to witness the arrival. "Here comes the great Mr. Gathergold!"

A carriage, drawn by four horses, dashed round the turn of the road. Within it, thrust partly out of the window, appeared the physiognomy of a little old man, with a skin as yellow as if his own Midas-hand had transmuted it. He had a low forehead, small, sharp eyes, puckered about with innumerable wrinkles, and very thin lips, which he made still thinner by pressing them forcibly together.

"The very image of the Great Stone Face!" shouted the people. "Sure enough, the old prophecy is true; and here we have the great man come, at last!"

And, what greatly perplexed Ernest, they seemed actually to believe that here was the likeness which they spoke of. By the roadside there chanced to be an old beggar-woman and two little beggar-children, stragglers from some far-off region, who, as the carriage rolled onward, held out their hands and lifted up their doleful voices, most piteously beseeching charity. A yellow claw- the very same that had clawed together so much wealth—poked itself out of the coach-window, and dropped some copper coins upon the ground; so that, though the great man's name seems to have been Gathergold, he might just as suitably have been nicknamed Scattercopper. Still, nevertheless, with an earnest shout, and evidently with as much good faith as ever, the people bellowed, "He is the very image of the Great Stone Face!"

But Ernest turned sadly from the wrinkled shrewdness of that sordid visage, and gazed up the valley, where, amid a gathering mist, gilded by the last sunbeams, he could still distinguish those glorious features which had impressed themselves into his soul. Their aspect cheered him. What did the benign lips seem to say?

"He will come! Fear not, Ernest; the man will come!"

The years went on, and Ernest ceased to be a boy. He had grown to be a young man now. He attracted little notice from the other inhabitants of the valley; for they saw nothing remarkable in his way of life, save that, when the labor of the day was over, he still loved to go apart and gaze and meditate upon the Great Stone Face. According to their idea of the matter, it was a folly, indeed, but pardonable, inasmuch as Ernest was industrious, kind, and neighborly, and neglected no duty for the sake of indulging this idle habit. They knew not that the Great Stone Face had become a teacher to him, and that the sentiment which was expressed in it would enlarge the young man's heart, and fill it with wider and deeper sympathies than other hearts. They knew not that thence would come a better wisdom than could be learned from books, and a better life than could be moulded on the defaced example of other human lives. Neither did Ernest know that the thoughts and affections which came to him so naturally, in the fields and at the fireside, and wherever he communed with himself, were of a higher tone than those which all men shared with him. A simple soul—simple as when his mother first taught him the old prophecy—he beheld the marvelous features beaming adown the valley, and still wondered that their human counterpart was so long in making his appearance.

By this time poor Mr. Gathergold was dead and buried; and the oddest part of the matter was, that his wealth, which was the body and spirit of his existence, had disappeared before his death, leaving nothing of him but a living skeleton, covered over with a wrinkled, yellow skin. Since the melting away of his gold, it had been very generally conceded that there was no such striking resemblance, after all, betwixt the ignoble features of the ruined merchant and that majestic face upon the mountain-side. So the people ceased to honor him during his lifetime, and quietly consigned him to forgetfulness after his decease. Once in a while, it is true, his memory was brought up in connection with the magnificent palace which he had built, and which had long ago been turned into a hotel for the accommodation of strangers, multitudes of whom came, every summer, to visit that famous natural curiosity, the Great Stone Face. Thus, Mr. Gathergold being discredited and thrown into the shade, the man of prophecy was yet to come.

It so happened that a native-born son of the valley, many years before, had enlisted as a soldier, and, after a great deal of hard fighting, had now become an illustrious commander. Whatever he may be called in history, he was known in camps and on the battle-field under the nickname of Old Blood-and-Thunder. This war-worn veteran, being now infirm with age and wounds, and weary of the turmoil of a military life, and of the roll of the drum and the clangor of the trumpet, that had so long been ringing in his ears, had lately signified a purpose of returning to his native valley, hoping to find repose where he remembered to have left it. The inhabitants, his old neighbors and their grown-up children, were resolved to welcome the renowned warrior with a salute of cannon and a public dinner; and all the more enthusiastically, it being affirmed that now, at last, the likeness of the Great Stone Face had actually appeared. An aid-de-camp of Old Blood-and-Thunder, traveling through the valley, was said to have been struck with the resemblance. Moreover, the schoolmates and early acquaintances of the general were ready to testify, on oath, that, to the best of their recollection, the aforesaid general had been exceedingly like the majestic image, even when a boy, only that the idea had never occurred to them at that period. Great, therefore, was the excitement throughout the valley; and many people, who had never once thought of glancing at the Great Stone Face for years before, now spent their time in gazing at it, for the sake of knowing exactly how General Blood-and-Thunder looked.

On the day of the great festival, Ernest, with all the other people of the valley, left their work, and proceeded to the spot where the sylvan banquet was prepared. As he approached, the loud voice of the Reverend Doctor Battleblast was heard, beseeching a blessing on the good things set before them, and on the distinguished friend of peace in whose honor they were assembled. The tables were arranged in a cleared space of the woods, shut in by the surrounding trees, except where a vista opened eastward, and afforded a distant view of the Great Stone Face. Over the general's chair, which was a relic from the home of Washington, there was an arch of verdant boughs, with the laurel profusely intermixed, and surmounted by his country's banner, beneath which he had won his victories. Our friend Ernest raised himself on his tip-toes, in hopes to get a glimpse of the celebrated guest; but there was a mighty crowd about the tables anxious to hear the toasts and speeches, and to catch any word that might fall from the general in reply; and a volunteer company, doing duty as a guard, pricked ruthlessly with their bayonets at any particularly quiet person among the throng. So Ernest, being of an unobtrusive character, was thrust quite into the background, where he could see no more of Old Blood-and-Thunder's physiognomy than if it had been still blazing on the battle-field. To console himself, he turned towards the Great Stone Face, which, like a faithful and long-remembered friend, looked back and smiled upon him through the vista of the forest. Meantime, however, he could over-hear the remarks of various individuals, who were comparing the features of the hero with the face on the distant mountain-side.

"'Tis the same face, to a hair!" cried one man, cutting a caper for joy.

"Wonderfully like, that's a fact!" responded another.

"Like! why, I call it Old Blood-and-Thunder himself, in a monstrous looking-glass!" cried a third. "And why not! He's the greatest man of this or any other age, beyond a doubt."

And then all three of the speakers gave a great shout, which communicated electricity to the crowd, and called forth a roar from a thousand voices, that went reverberating for miles among the mountains, until you might have supposed that the Great Stone Face had poured its thunder-breath into the cry. All these comments, and this vast enthusiasm, served the more to interest our friend; nor did he think of questioning that now, at length, the mountain-visage had found its human counterpart. It is true, Ernest had imagined that this long-looked-for personage would appear in the character of a man of peace, uttering wisdom, and doing good, and making people happy. But, taking an habitual breadth of view, with all his simplicity, he contended that Providence should choose its own method of blessing mankind, and could conceive that this great end might be effected even by a warrior and a bloody sword, should inscrutable wisdom see fit to order matters so.

"The general! the general!" was now the cry. "Hush! silence! Old Blood-and-Thunder's going to make a speech."

Even so; for, the cloth being removed, the general's health had been drunk amid shouts of applause, and he now stood upon his feet to thank the company. Ernest saw him. There he was, over the shoulders of the crowd, from the two glittering epaulets and embroidered collar upward, beneath the arch of green boughs with inter-twined laurel and the banner drooping as if to shade his brow! And there, too, visible in the same glance, through the vista of the forest, appeared the Great Stone Face! And was there, indeed, such a resemblance as the crowd had testified? Alas, Ernest could not recognize it! He beheld a war-worn and weather-beaten countenance, full of energy, and expressive of an iron will; but the gentle wisdom, the deep, broad, tender sympathies, were altogether wanting in Old Blood-and-Thunder's visage; and even if the Great Stone Face had assumed his look of stern command, the milder traits would still have tempered it.

"This is not the man of prophecy," sighed Ernest to himself, as he made his way out of the throng. "And must the world wait longer yet?"

The mists had congregated about the distant mountain-side, and there were seen the grand and awful features of the Great Stone Face, awful but benignant, as if a mighty angel were sitting among the hills, and enrobing himself

in a cloud-vesture of gold and purple. As he looked, Ernest
could hardly believe but that a smile beamed over the
whole visage, with a radiance still brightening, although
without motion of the lips. It was probably the effect of
the western sunshine, melting through the thinly diffused
vapors that had swept between him and the object that
he gazed at. But—as it always did—the aspect of his
marvelous friend made Ernest as hopeful as if he had
never hoped in vain.

"Fear not, Ernest," said his heart, even as if the Great Face
were whispering him, "fear not, Ernest; he will come."

More years sped swiftly and tranquilly away. Ernest still
dwelt in his native valley, and was now a man of middle
age. By imperceptible degrees, he had become known
among the people. Now, as heretofore, he labored for his
bread, and was the same simple-hearted man that he had
always been. But he had thought and felt so much, he had
given so many of the best hours of his life to unworldly
hopes for some great good to mankind, that it seemed
as though he had been talking with the angels, and had
imbibed a portion of their wisdom unawares. It was visible
in the calm and well-considered beneficence of his daily
life, the quiet stream of which had made a wide green
margin all along its course. Not a day passed by, that the
world was not the better because this man, humble as
he was, had lived. He never stepped aside from his own
path, yet would always reach a blessing to his neighbor.
Almost involuntarily, too, he had become a preacher. The
pure and high simplicity of his thought, which, as one
of its manifestations, took shape in the good deeds that
dropped silently from his hand, flowed also forth in
speech. He uttered truths that wrought upon and moulded
the lives of those who heard him. His auditors, it may
be, never suspected that Ernest, their own neighbor and
familiar friend, was more than an ordinary man; least of
all did Ernest himself suspect it; but, inevitably as the
murmur of a rivulet, came thoughts out of his mouth that
no other human lips had spoken.

When the people's minds had had a little time to cool,
they were ready enough to acknowledge their mistake
in imagining a similarity between General Blood-and-
Thunder's truculent physiognomy and the benign visage
on the mountain-side. But now, again, there were reports
and many paragraphs in the newspapers, affirming that
the likeness of the Great Stone Face had appeared upon

the broad shoulders of a certain eminent statesman. He, like Mr. Gathergold and Old Blood-and-Thunder, was a native of the valley, but had left it in his early days, and taken up the trades of law and politics. Instead of the rich man's wealth and the warrior's sword, he had but a tongue, and it was mightier than both together. So wonderfully eloquent was he, that whatever he might choose to say, his auditors had no choice but to believe him; wrong looked like right, and right like wrong; for when it pleased him, he could make a kind of illuminated fog with his mere breath, and obscure the natural daylight with it. His tongue, indeed, was a magic instrument: sometimes it rumbled like the thunder; sometimes it warbled like the sweetest music. It was the blast of war- the song of peace; and it seemed to have a heart in it, when there was no such matter. In good truth, he was a wondrous man; and when his tongue had acquired him all other imaginable success— when it had been heard in halls of state, and in the courts of princes and potentates—after it had made him known all over the world, even as a voice crying from shore to shore—it finally persuaded his countrymen to select him for the presidency. Before this time—indeed, as soon as he began to grow celebrated—his admirers had found out the resemblance between him and the Great Stone Face; and so much were they struck by it, that throughout the country this distinguished gentleman was known by the name of Old Stony Phiz. The phrase was considered as giving a highly favorable aspect to his political prospects; for, as is likewise the case with the Popedom, nobody ever becomes president without taking a name other than his own.

While his friends were doing their best to make him president, Old Stony Phiz, as he was called, set out on a visit to the valley where he was born. Of course, he had no other object than to shake hands with his fellow-citizens, and neither thought nor cared about any effect which his progress through the country might have upon the election. Magnificent preparations were made to receive the illustrious statesman; a cavalcade of horsemen set forth to meet him at the boundary line of the state, and all the people left their business and gathered along the wayside to see him pass. Among these was Ernest. Though more than once disappointed, as we have seen, he had such a hopeful and confiding nature, that he was always ready to believe in whatever seemed beautiful and good. He kept his heart continually open, and thus was sure to catch the blessing from on high, when it should come. So now again, as buoyantly as ever, he went forth to behold the likeness of the Great Stone Face.

The cavalcade came prancing along the road, with a great clattering of hoofs and a mighty cloud of dust, which rose up so dense and high that the visage of the mountain-side was completely hidden from Ernest's eyes. All the great men of the neighborhood were there on horseback: militia officers, in uniform; the member of Congress; the sheriff of the county; the editors of newspapers; and many a farmer, too, had mounted his patient steed, with his Sunday coat upon his back. It really was a very brilliant spectacle, especially as there were numerous banners flaunting over the cavalcade, on some of which were gorgeous portraits of the illustrious statesman and the Great Stone Face, smiling familiarly at one another, like two brothers. If the pictures were to be trusted, the mutual resemblance, it must be confessed, was marvelous. We must not forget to mention that there was a band of music, which made the echoes of the mountains ring and reverberate with the loud triumph of its strains; so that airy and soul-thrilling melodies broke out among all the heights and hollows as if every nook of his native valley had found a voice to welcome the distinguished guest. But the grandest effect was when the far-off mountain-precipice flung back the music; for then the Great Stone Face itself seemed to be swelling the triumphant chorus, in acknowledgment that, at length, the man of prophecy was come.

All this while the people were throwing up their hats and shouting, with enthusiasm so contagious that the heart of Ernest kindled up, and he likewise threw up his hat, and shouted, as loudly as the loudest, "Huzza for the great man! Huzza for Old Stony Phiz!" But as yet he had not seen him.

"Here he is, now!" cried those who stood near Ernest. "There! There! Look at Old Stony Phiz and then at the Old Man of the Mountain, and see if they are not as like as two twin-brothers!"

In the midst of all this gallant array, came an open barouche, drawn by four white horses; and in the barouche, with his massive head uncovered, sat the illustrious statesman, Old Stony Phiz himself.

"Confess it," said one of Ernest's neighbors to him, "the Great Stone Face has met its match at last!"

Now, it must be owned that, at his first glimpse of the countenance which was bowing and smiling from the barouche, Ernest did fancy that there was a resemblance between it and the old familiar face upon the mountainside. The brow, with its massive depth and loftiness, and all the other features, indeed, were boldly and strongly hewn, as if in emulation of a more than heroic, of a Titanic model. But the sublimity and stateliness, the grand expression of a divine sympathy, that illuminated the mountain-visage, and etherealized its ponderous granite substance into spirit, might here be sought in vain. Something had been originally left out, or had departed. And therefore the marvelously gifted statesman had always a weary gloom in the deep caverns of his eyes, as of a child that has outgrown its playthings, or a man of mighty faculties and little aims, whose life, with all its high performances, was vague and empty, because no high purpose had endowed it with reality.

Still, Ernest's neighbor was thrusting his elbow into his side, and pressing him for an answer.

"Confess! confess! Is not he the very picture of your Old Man of the Mountain?"

"No!" said Ernest, bluntly, "I see little or no likeness."

"Then so much the worse for the Great Stone Face!" answered his neighbor; and again he set up a shout for Old Stony Phiz.

But Ernest turned away. melancholy, and almost despondent; for this was the saddest of his disappointments, to behold a man who might have fulfilled the prophecy, and had not willed to do so. Meantime, the cavalcade, the banners, the music, and the barouches, swept past him, with the vociferous crowd in the rear, leaving the dust to settle down, and the Great Stone Face to be revealed again, with the grandeur that it had worn for untold centuries.

"Lo, here I am, Ernest!" the benign lips seemed to say. "I have waited longer than thou, and am not yet weary. Fear not; the man will come."

The years hurried onward, treading in their haste on one another's heels. And now they began to bring white hairs, and scatter them over the head of Ernest; they made reverend wrinkles across his forehead, and furrows in his cheeks. He was an aged man. But not in vain had he grown old: more than the white hairs on his head were the sage thoughts in his mind; his wrinkles and furrows were inscriptions that Time had graved, and in which he had written legends of wisdom that had been

tested by the tenor of a life. And Ernest had ceased to
be obscure. Unsought for, undesired, had come the fame
which so many seek, and made him known in the great
world, beyond the limits of the valley in which he had
dwelt so quietly. College professors, and even the active
men of cities, came from far to see and converse with
Ernest; for the report had gone abroad that this simple
husbandman had ideas unlike those of other men, not
gained from books, but of a higher tone—a tranquil and
familiar majesty, as if he had been talking with the angels
as his daily friends. Whether it were sage, statesman, or
philanthropist, Ernest received these visitors with the
gentle sincerity that had characterized him from boyhood,
and spoke freely with them of whatever came uppermost,
or lay deepest in his heart or their own. While they talked
together, his face would kindle, unawares, and shine
upon them, as with a mild evening light. Pensive with the
fulness of such discourse, his guests took leave and went
their way; and, passing up the valley, paused to look at the
Great Stone Face, imagining that they had seen its likeness
in a human countenance, but could not remember where.

While Ernest had been growing up and growing old, a
bountiful Providence had granted a new poet to this earth.
He, likewise, was a native of the valley but had spent the
greater part of his life at a distance from that romantic
region, pouring out his sweet music amid the bustle and
din of cities. Often, however, did the mountains which
had been familiar to him in his childhood lift their snowy
peaks into the clear atmosphere of his poetry. Neither was
the Great Stone Face forgotten, for the poet had celebrated
it in an ode, which was grand enough to have been uttered
by its own majestic lips. This man of genius, we may say,
had come down from heaven with wonderful endowments.
If he sang of a mountain, the eyes of all mankind beheld
a mightier grandeur reposing on its breast, or soaring
to its summit, than had before been seen there. If his
theme were a lovely lake, a celestial smile had now been
thrown over it, to gleam forever on its surface. If it were
the vast old sea, even the deep immensity of its dread
bosom seemed to swell the higher, as if moved by the
emotions of the song. Thus the world assumed another
and a better aspect from the hour that the poet blessed it
with his happy eyes. The Creator had bestowed him, as the
last, best touch to his own handiwork. Creation was not
finished till the poet came to interpret, and so complete it.

The effect was no less high and beautiful, when his
human brethren were the subject of his verse. The man
or woman, sordid with the common dust of life, who
crossed his daily path, and the little child who played in

it, were glorified if he beheld them in his mood of poetic faith. He showed the golden links of the great chain that intertwined them with an angelic kindred; he brought out the hidden traits of a celestial birth that made them worthy of such kin. Some, indeed, there were, who thought to show the soundness of their judgment by affirming that all the beauty and dignity of the natural world existed only in the poet's fancy. Let such men speak for themselves, who undoubtedly appear to have been spawned forth by Nature with a contemptuous bitterness; she having plastered them up out of her refuse stuff, after all the swine were made. As respects all things else, the poet's ideal was the truest truth.

The songs of this poet found their way to Ernest. He read them, after his customary toil, seated on the bench before his cottage door, where, for such a length of time, he had filled his repose with thought by gazing at the Great Stone Face. And now, as he read stanzas that caused the soul to thrill within him, he lifted his eyes to the vast countenance beaming on him so benignantly.

"O, majestic friend," he murmured, addressing the Great Stone Face, "is not this man worthy to resemble thee?"

The Face seemed to smile, but answered not a word.

Now it happened that the poet, though he dwelt so far away, had not only heard of Ernest, but had meditated much upon his character, until he deemed nothing so desirable as to meet this man, whose untaught wisdom walked hand in hand with the noble simplicity of his life. One summer morning, therefore, he took passage by the railroad, and, in the decline of the afternoon, alighted from the cars at no great distance from Ernest's cottage. The great hotel, which had formerly been the palace of Mr. Gathergold, was close at hand, but the poet with his carpet-bag on his arm, inquired at once where Ernest dwelt, and was resolved to be accepted as his guest.

Approaching the door, he there found the good old man, holding a volume in his hand, which alternately he read, and then, with a finger between the leaves, looked lovingly at the Great Stone Face.

"Good evening," said the poet. "Can you give a traveller a night's lodging?"'

"Willingly," answered Ernest; and then he added, smiling, "Methinks I never saw the Great Stone Face look so hospitably at a stranger."

The poet sat down on the bench beside him, and he and Ernest talked together. Often had the poet held intercourse with the wittiest and the wisest, but never before with a man like Ernest, whose thoughts and feelings gushed up with such a natural freedom, and who made great truths so familiar by his simple utterance of them. Angels, as had been so often said, seemed to have wrought with him at his labor in the fields; angels seemed to have sat with him by the fireside; and, dwelling with angels as friend with friends, he had imbibed the sublimity of their ideas, and imbued it with the sweet and lowly charm of household words. So thought the poet. And Ernest, on the other hand, was moved and agitated by the living images which the poet flung out of his mind, and which peopled all the air about the cottage-door with shapes of beauty, both gay and pensive. The sympathies of these two men instructed them with a profounder sense than either could have attained alone. Their minds accorded into one strain, and made delightful music which neither of them could have claimed as all his own, nor distinguished his own share from the other's. They led one another, as it were, into a high pavilion of their thoughts, so remote, and hitherto so dim, that they had never entered it before, and so beautiful that they desired to be

there always.

As Ernest listened to the poet, he imagined that the Great Stone Face was bending forward to listen too. He gazed earnestly into the poet's glowing eyes.

"Who are you, my strangely gifted guest?" he said.

The poet laid his finger on the volume that Ernest had been reading.

"You have read these poems," said he. "You know me, then—for I wrote them."

Again, and still more earnestly than before, Ernest examined the poet's features; then turned towards the Great Stone Face; then back, with an uncertain aspect, to his guest. But his countenance fell; he shook his head, and sighed.

"Wherefore are you sad?" inquired the poet.

"Because, replied Ernest, "all through life I have awaited the fulfilment of a prophecy; and, when I read these poems, I hoped that it might be fulfilled in you."

"You hoped," answered the poet, faintly smiling, "to find in me the likeness of the Great Stone Face. And you are disappointed, as formerly with Mr. Gathergold, and Old Blood-and-Thunder, and Old Stony Phiz. Yes, Ernest, it is my doom. You must add my name to the illustrious three, and record another failure of your hopes. For—in shame and sadness do I speak it, Ernest—I am not worthy to be typified by yonder benign and majestic image."

"And why?" asked Ernest. He pointed to the volume—
"Are not those thoughts divine?"

"They have a strain of the Divinity," replied the poet.
"You can hear in them the far-off echo of a heavenly song.
But my life, dear Ernest, has not corresponded with my
thought. I have had grand dreams, but they have been
only dreams, because I have lived—and that, too, by
own choice—among poor and mean realities. Sometimes
even—shall I dare to say it?—I lack faith in the grandeur,
the beauty, and the goodness, which my own works are
said to have made more evident in nature and in human
life. Why, then, pure seeker of the good and true, shouldst
thou hope to find me, in yonder image of the divine!"

The poet spoke sadly, and his eyes were dim with tears.
So, likewise, were those of Ernest.

At the hour of sunset, as had long been his frequent
custom, Ernest was to discourse to an assemblage of
the neighboring inhabitants, in the open air. He and the
poet, arm in arm, still talking together as they went along,
proceeded to the spot. It was a small nook among the hills,
with a gray precipice behind, the stern front of which was
relieved by the pleasant foliage of many creeping plants,
that made a tapestry for the naked rock, by hanging their
festoons from all its rugged angles. At a small elevation
above the ground, set in a rich frame-work of verdure,
there appeared a niche, spacious enough to admit a human
figure, with freedom for such gestures as spontaneously
accompany earnest thought and genuine emotion. Into
this natural pulpit Ernest ascended, and threw a look of
familiar kindness around upon his audience. They stood,
or sat, or reclined upon the grass, as seemed good to each,
with the departing sunshine falling obliquely over them,
and mingling its subdued cheerfulness with the solemnity
of a grove of ancient trees, beneath and amid the boughs
of which the golden rays were constrained to pass. In
another direction was seen the Great Stone Face, with the
same cheer, combined with the same solemnity, in its
benignant aspect.

Ernest began to speak, giving to the people of what was
in his heart and mind. His words had power, because they
accorded with his thoughts; and his thoughts had reality
and depth, because they harmonized with the life which he
had always lived. It was not mere breath that this preacher
uttered; they were the words of life, because a life of
good deeds and holy love was melted into them. Pearls,
pure and rich, had been dissolved into this precious
draught. The poet, as he listened, felt that the being and
character of Ernest were a nobler strain of poetry than he

had ever written. His eyes glistening with tears, he gazed reverentially at the venerable man, and said within himself that never was there an aspect so worthy of a prophet and a sage as that mild, sweet, thoughtful countenance, with the glory of white hair diffused about it. At a distance, but distinctly to be seen, high up in the golden light of the setting sun, appeared the Great Stone Face, with hoary mists around it, like the white hairs around the brow of Ernest. Its look of grand beneficence seemed to embrace the world.

At that moment, in sympathy with a thought which he was about to utter, the face of Ernest assumed a grandeur of expression, so imbued with benevolence, that the poet, by an irresistible impulse, threw his arms aloft, and shouted, "Behold! Behold! Ernest is himself the likeness of the Great Stone Face!"

Then all the people looked, and saw that what the deep-sighted poet said was true. The prophecy was fulfilled. But Ernest, having finished what he had to say, took the poet's arm, and walked slowly homeward, still hoping that some wiser and better man than himself would by and by appear, bearing a resemblance to the GREAT STONE FACE.

ABOUT THE AUTHOR

Steve Demme and his wife Sandra have been married since 1979. They have been blessed with four sons, three lovely daughters-in-law, and three special grandchildren.

Steve has served in full or part time pastoral ministry for many years after graduating from Gordon-Conwell Theological Seminary. He is the creator of Math-U-See and the founder of Building Faith Familie.

He produces a monthly newsletter, weekly podcasts, and regular posts facebook.com/stevedemme/

Steve is a regular speaker at home education conferences, men's ministry events, and family retreats. His desire is to strengthen, teach, encourage, validate, and exhort parents and families to follow the biblical model for the Christian home

BUILDING FAITH FAMILIES

Exists to teach and encourage families to embrace the biblical model for the Christian home.

Scripture declares God created the sacred institution of the family. In His wisdom, He designed marriage to be between one man and one woman. We believe healthy God-fearing families are the basic building block for the church and society.

The family is foundational and transformational. Parents and children become more like Jesus as they lay their lives down for each other, pray for each other, and learn to love each other as God has loved them.

RESOURCES TO ENCOURAGE AND STRENGTHEN YOUR FAMILY

The Monthly Newsletter

- This an encouraging exhortation as well as updates on Bible contests and upcoming speaking engagements.

Podcast

- Each week a new episode is released on our website, Itunes, and our Facebook page. These may be downloaded for free.

Seminars for free download

- For over 30 years Steve has been speaking and teaching at conferences around the world. Many of his messages are available for your edification.

MORE BUILDING FAITH
FAMILY RESOURCES

CRISIS TO CHRIST

THE HARDEST AND BEST YEAR OF MY LIFE

I have wounds, scars, baggage, and stuff from my past, which I have tried to ignore, but which is always present. In 2012 I was confronted with the distressing knowledge that my own wounds, which I thought were hidden and of no consequence, were wounding those closest to me, my wife and sons. I discovered I cannot hide my toxic issues for eventually they will leak out and hurt those who are closest to me, primarily my wife and children.

This difficult time, the hardest and best year of my life, was instrumental in changing my life and transforming my relationship with God and my family. On this journey I experienced pain which led me to acknowledge my own hurts and get help from the body of Christ to understand root causes of my distress and confront unbiblical thinking.

While I experienced incredible pain, I also discovered that my Heavenly Dad likes me just the way I am. Even though my path went through deep waters, God was with me every step of the way.

My motivation in writing is to affirm others who are going through similar valleys and tribulations. These hard journeys are normal for the Christian. Every person of note in scripture endured at least one life changing crisis. God uses these difficult times to work deep in our hearts, reveal more of Himself, and transform us into the image of His Son.

KNOWING GOD'S LOVE,

BECOMING ROOTED AND GROUNDED IN GRACE

Comprehending God's unconditional love is the cornerstone for the overarching commands to love God and our neighbor. For we are unable to love until we have first been loved. "We love, because He first loved us." (1 John 4:19) and "In this is love, not that we have loved God but that he loved us." (1 John 4:10)

The first, or as Jesus called it, the Great Command, is to love God. I began asking God to help me love Him with all my heart, soul, mind, and strength and was wonderfully surprised by how he answered my request.

Instead of awaking one morning with a burning love for God, which I expected, He began to steadily reveal how much He loved me. In 2012 I found myself believing in a new way that God knows me thoroughly and loves me completely. This knowledge that God likes me for who I am, and not based on what I do, has transformed my life.

As I have become more rooted and grounded in grace, my relationship with God is now much richer and deeper. My wife and I are closer than we have ever been. Knowing I am loved and accepted just as I am, has freed me to be more transparent and real as I relate with my sons and others.

FAMILY WORSHIP

In this readable and encouraging book, Steve shares practical scripture–based tips for teaching the word of God to children of all ages.

He also addresses common obstacles we all face in establishing the discipline of regular family worship. Be encouraged by Steve's experiences teaching his four sons, and learn from other families who share strategies that have worked for their children. You may purchase this book, or participate in our Family Worship Challenge. When you read or listen to "The Christian Home and Family Worship" within 30 days of receiving your copy, it is yours for FREE. If you are unable to fulfill this obligation, you agree to send a check for $50.00 to Building Faith Families.

Steve will follow up with you at the end of thirty days. Contact Steve at sdemme@ demmelearning.com

"I loved the book and read it in about a week and a half. My chief take-away was family worship needs to be an important part of family life. I've had five family worship times and I can definitely say I've already seen some fruits from these sessions. Your book had some great examples of how to make it more appealing to the kids."

"I was indeed able to read the book in time. The main thing I took away from it was the Nike slogan: "Just do it." So I did.

SPEAKING THE TRUTH IN LOVE

LESSONS I'VE LEARNED ABOUT
FAMILY COMMUNICATION

Most of what I've learned about communication, I acquired in the past few years during transitioning my business to a family owned business. The ability to communicate about difficult topics like business, values, your occupation, and a family's legacy takes effort and training.

As a husband and father, I have the potential to build up and encourage my family like no one else. I also have the ability to tear down and discourage my wife and sons. The Bible teaches effective principles of communication which are timeless.

My relationship with my wife and children has been transformed through godly safe communication. As I continue to grow in grace and the knowledge of God, I am in a better place to have open, transparent, and honest communication. While the skills we have acquired in being a clear speaker and an engaged listener are beneficial, investing time to have a quiet heart is essential. For out of the abundance of the heart, the mouth speaks.

I hope the principles we have learned and applied to such benefit in our own home and business will be a help to you on your journey. May the words of our mouth and the meditation of our heart be acceptable in your sight, O LORD, our Rock and our Redeemer. (from Psalms 19:14)

STEWARDSHIP

"Where your treasure is, there will your heart be also." (Luke 12:34)

Stewardship is personal finance taught from a biblical perspective, written by the author of the successful Math-U-See curriculum, Steve Demme. With his signature humility, humor, and sharp math skills, Steve combines practical math instruction with Biblical principles of finance and discipleship material.

It is appropriate for anyone with a good understanding of math and beginning algebra. Many parents have commented they wish they had this class when they were a young adult.

This new revision is updated with current topics relevant to young people aged 15-17, who are beginning to explore more independent financial opportunities and responsibilities. Here is a sampling of the thirty-six topics

Consumer Math Topics

- Banking & Checking
- Budgeting & Credit Cards
- Cost of Owning a Vehicle
- Understanding Mortgages
- Medical Insurance and Bearing Burdens
- Cost of Post Secondary Education
- Entrepreneur
- Christian Micro-Finance
- Compound Interest and Investing

Since the heart is connected to our treasure, it is essential to nurture our heart from God's inspired Word. In each of the thirty-six lesson there devotional material called *Biblical Principles and Scripture Studies*. These focus on Biblical principles of finance as well as Scripture studies on basic discipleship. Here is a sampling.

Biblical Principles to Govern Our Treasure

- The Love of Money
- Trusting God and Being Content
- Honor the Lord With Your Wealth
- Giving From a Redeemed Heart
- The Poor, Widows and Orphans
- The Blessing of God

Scripture Studies to Instruct Our Heart

- Loving God and Belonging to God
- Conviction Versus Condemnation
- The First Commandment With a Promise
- David, a Man After God's Heart
- The Ministry and Work of the Spirit
- Jesus, the Suffering Servant Our Identity in Jesus

The *Student Workbook* has thirty-six lessons are organized into a weekly format, with five worksheets per lesson. There are ten questions per lesson. Seven problems are from consumer math topics, two are from the Biblical Principles and Scripture Studies, and one is written to facilitate family discussion.

HYMNS FOR FAMILY WORSHIP

This time-honored collection of 100 classic hymns will be a rich addition to your family worship. Make a joyful noise to the LORD!

In addition to the music for these carefully selected songs of worship, the history and origin of each hymn enhances the meaning of the lyrics.

There are four CDs with piano accompaniment for singing along in your home, car, or church.

Some of the titles are:
- What a Friend We Have in Jesus
- Holy, Holy, Holy
- It Is Well With My Soul
- To God Be The Glory
- All Hail the Power of Jesus Name
- Amazing Grace
- How Firm a Foundation
- Blessed Assurance
- Christ Arose
- Rise Up O Men of God
- Jesus Paid It All
- Just As I Am, along with 88 more!